LAUREN BACALL

HER FILMS
AND CAREER

BY LAWRENCE J. QUIRK

The Citadel Press   Secaucus, New Jersey

BOOKS BY LAWRENCE J. QUIRK

THE FILMS OF JOAN CRAWFORD
ROBERT FRANCIS KENNEDY
THE FILMS OF INGRID BERGMAN
THE FILMS OF PAUL NEWMAN
THE FILMS OF FREDRIC MARCH
PHOTOPLAY ANTHOLOGY (Wrote Foreword)
THE FILMS OF WILLIAM HOLDEN
THE GREAT ROMANTIC FILMS
THE FILMS OF ROBERT TAYLOR
SOME LOVELY IMAGE (A Novel)
THE FILMS OF RONALD COLMAN
THE FILMS OF WARREN BEATTY
THE FILMS OF MYRNA LOY
THE FILMS OF GLORIA SWANSON
CLAUDETTE COLBERT: AN ILLUSTRATED BIOGRAPHY
BETTE DAVIS: HER FILMS AND CAREER (Update since 1965)
JANE WYMAN: THE WOMAN AND THE ACTRESS
LAUREN BACALL: HER FILMS AND CAREER

FOR ALLAN J. WILSON AND LYLE STUART

Co-Winners in 1982 of the Eighteenth James R. Quirk Award, for editing and publishing historically valuable books that have rendered an immensely fruitful service to the art of film and its traditions.

Designed by Lester Glassner

Published by Citadel Press
A division of Lyle Stuart, Inc.
120 Enterprise Avenue, Secaucus, N.J. 07094

In Canada: Musson Book Company
A division of General Publishing Co. Limited
Don Mills, Ontario

Manufactured in the United States of America

Library of Congress Cataloging-in-Publication Data

Quirk, Lawrence J.
  Lauren Bacall : her films and career.

  1. Bacall, Lauren, 1924-   .   2. Actors—United
States—Biography. I. Title.
PN2287.B115Q57 1986 791.43′028′0924 [B] 86-2310
ISBN 0-8065-0935-X

ACKNOWLEDGMENTS

Again my warm thanks to Douglas Whitney, for his loan of many rare and valuable pictures of Miss Lauren Bacall. Also thanks to Ernest D. Burns and Cinemabilia, New York; Mark Ricci and the Memory Shop, New York; Jerry Ohlinger and his Movie Material Store, New York; Philip Lyman and the Gotham Book Mart, New York; Dorothy Swerdlove and Dr. Rod Bladel and the staff of the New York Public Library's Theatre and Film Collection, Library and Museum of Performing Arts, New York; Academy of Motion Picture Arts & Sciences, Los Angeles; and Warner Bros., Twentieth Century-Fox, Universal, United Artists, MGM-UA, NBC-TV, Paramount, CBS-TV, ABC-TV and the many individuals at these firms and in private life who, without wishing to be named, generously shared with me their memories of Miss Bacall.

Also my appreciation to James E. Runyan, William Schoell, Michael Ritzer, John A. Guzman, Arthur Tower, Mike Snell, Don Koll, John Cocchi, Neal Peters, Doug McClelland, Albert B. Manski, Frank Rowley, Howard Otway, Fredda Dudley Balling, Paul and Helen Denis, Jim McGowan, DeWitt Bodeen, Martin Sopocy, Andrew Achsen, Ben Carbonetto, Manuel Cordova, Eduardo Moreno, George Geltzer, and Adam Scull/Globe Photos.

CONTENTS

	page
Lauren Bacall: Her Life	9
A Lauren Bacall Portrait Gallery	31
The Films	59
To Have and Have Not *1944*	60
Confidential Agent *1945*	68
Two Guys from Milwaukee *1946*	74
The Big Sleep *1946*	77
Dark Passage *1947*	84
Key Largo *1948*	91
Young Man With a Horn *1950*	97
Bright Leaf *1950*	105
How to Marry a Millionaire *1953*	110
Woman's World *1954*	120
The Cobweb *1955*	127
Blood Alley *1955*	133
Written on the Wind *1956*	138
Designing Woman *1957*	144
The Gift of Love *1958*	149
Flame Over India *1960*	154
Shock Treatment *1964*	159
Sex and the Single Girl *1964*	164
Harper *1966*	168
Murder on the Orient Express *1974*	171
The Shootist *1976*	178
The Fan *1981*	182
Health *1982*	190

LAUREN BACALL: *HER LIFE*

Lauren Bacall celebrates her 62nd birthday on September 16, 1986—and some sixty-two years it has been! And on October 11 of 1986 she officially celebrates her forty-second anniversary as a film personality. For that was the date in 1944 when her blockbusting initial movie, *To Have and Have Not,* opened in New York.

To Have and Have Not might well describe her long and turbulent existence—on screen, on stage, on television—throughout an up-and-down, fire-and-ice, great-success-and-great-failure, great-happiness-and-great-sorrow, *sturm-und-drang,* yang-and-ying life course, which highlighted, and for the whole country to witness, an assortment of vicissitudes, disillusionments, and variegated disasters that might have driven a weaker, less determined woman to suicide, drink, drugs, or any other escape mechanism that might have presented itself.

But Lauren Bacall is not a woman given to escapisms of any kind. "Whatever it is, face it," has always been one of her predominant life-maxims. "Face it! Head-on!"

Which probably explains why this gutsy, resilient, often abrasively forthright, consummately valorous person is one of Life's Great Survivors—In Spades.

Many people adore her—and, yes, many despise her. Some love her hang-in-there, wade-through-all-obstacles-unflinchingly, masculinely-tough approach to life's hurdles and traps. Others consider her vulgarly pushy, chutzpa-ishly brazen, mean as sin and inexorable in the attainment of whatever goal is currently firing her up. Her ready answer to such criticisms can be summed up as: "Let people push you around, and you deserve whatever bad things happen after that."

People who have gotten to know Bacall well cite her initial vulnerability, her youthful idealism and romanticism that made her Bette Davis's biggest fan circa 1939. She confirms this certainly on the opening page of her autobiography, *Lauren Bacall By Myself,* in which she wrote, "Bette Davis was my fifteen-year-old idea of perfection—fine actress, dramatic bravery, doomed tragedy, sardonic wit—all an actress should be, and when I cut school I would sit all day in a movie house sobbing through *Dark Victory* or *Jezebel* or *The Old Maid.*"

And when, through the courtesy of mutual friends, she and a girlfriend got to meet her goddess for tea one afternoon at a New York hotel, she described the encounter in one of her book's more rhapsodic and deeply-felt passages.

At the age of 10…already a model.

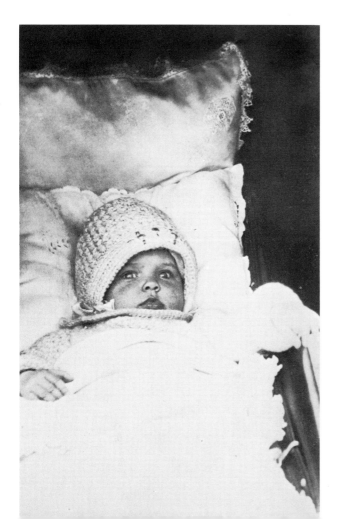

"Ruthless, yes," she was to say of herself many years later, "I admit to that. But I've got my human, tender side, believe it or not—if people deserve to be shown it."

Many sing the praises of Bacall's courage, fighting spirit, ability to survive, loyalty to family and close friends; and there are those who cite her tactlessness, prima-donnaism, bitchy cruelty, and outright scorn for people she considers unworthy of her attention—and these are many.

She is bitter about some things—bitter and unforgiving—and it could be she has her legitimate reasons. She is also passionately loyal and devoted to people—and causes—she cherishes. Among her steadfast beliefs: People who get to know too much about one use it *against* one; flaunt one's vulnerability and people drive in a knife.

Too sensible and realistic a woman for multiple-marriage marathons, she has been wed only twice in those sixty-two years—widowed once, divorced once—which says volumes for her mature restraint and common sense in private matters. She was a callow, green but already incandescent bright new star when she married, at 20, the 46-year-old Humphrey Bogart, one of the greatest stars the

As a baby.

screen was ever to boast. His paternal protectiveness and mellow life-experience greatly eased her passage into womanly maturity.

"In my eleven years as his wife [1945-1957] I knew the greatest happiness of my life," she has said. "I have never known quite that quality of pure happiness since." Four years after Bogart's death, she married, in 1961, another great star, Jason Robards, Jr.; he was 39, she was 36. Robards, a theatre luminary of the first magnitude, was and is an acting genius who has interpreted the characters of Eugene O'Neill as no one has before or since. Privately, he was and is a tormented man, burdened with oppressive alimony and child-support payments to former wives and children that have kept him permanently in near-bankruptcy, despite his fabulous earnings. He also drank excessively, and resented comparisons with Bacall's first husband, feeling that he was condemned to live in a dead man's shadow.

Result: a second marriage for Bacall that lasted only eight short years, ending when they realized that they had nothing to share any more.

Then there were the three children—two, Stephen and Leslie, by Bogart, and one, Sam, by Robards. They are 37, 34 and 24 respectively, as of 1986. Stephen, who went through painful initial flounderings in search for an identity other than as Humphrey Bogart's son, finally settled down into marriage and parenthood, and has made a career for himself in business. Daughter Leslie, a steady, sensible soul, became a nurse. And young Sam Robards, a sensitive young man who has undergone his own traumas as helpless witness to the deteriorating marriage of two parents he loved equally, seems at last to be laying his personal demons to rest in the pursuit of the acting profession they both inspired in him.

"I know my good and bad points, and I can live with them, God knows," Bacall has said, "but what really breaks my heart is that my innocent young ones have had to pay for my mistakes. On the whole, though, I think I have been a decent mother, and an attentive one, and there'll be, I'm sure, no *Mommie Dearest* trash written about *me* when I'm gone!"

Many Bacall aficionados feel that the failure of the Robards marriage was entirely his fault, and that she fought for eight years a game but losing battle to save it, given his drinking and complex quirks of character.

Then there were Bacall's stresses and bewildering ups-and-downs in her film career, which started off so brilliantly that fall of 1944, began floundering with her second picture, rose slightly, then dipped again, then settled down comfortably—then fizzled out almost entirely. Feeling, circa 1959, that superficial-minded, duplicitous Hollywood had no further use for her, the humiliated but determined Widow Bogart found a whole new success and acceptance—and warm appreciation—in the Broadway theatre, where she was to be accorded phenomenally long runs as one of its greatest stars—and where, in time, she was to find her great talent honored to the tune of several Tony Awards.

Outside of her marriages, she has never been lucky in her men. An early crush, in their New York youth, on Kirk Douglas went unreciprocated, though he was always to be her friend; then, after Bogart's death, a promising romantic start with Frank Sinatra fizzled disillusioningly when he walked out on her when she expressed her hopes for marriage and it broke in the press. "Frank was an odd combination of the greatest kindness and the greatest cruelty," she later said of him.

Other romantic disappointments with actors Len

In her modelling days. "The Look" by then was quite evident.

Cariou and Harry Guardino, who were her leading-men in her Broadway smashes *Applause* (1970) and *Woman of the Year* (1981), were to be her lot. Ditto a certain Englishman she was in love with during the 1970s who at first returned, then withdrew from, her love.

She has had her periodic bouts with financial trouble, which hard work for top earnings on the stage dissipated—for a time. She has lost those near and dear to her—her mother, other relatives, a beloved aide. Always she has managed to pick up the pieces of her life and go on.

Writer Joe Hyams, who knew Bacall and Bogart intimately and did a book on them, has quoted Bogart as recalling that it was her height that first intrigued him—that, and her cat-like grace. And a decade into the marriage, Bogart claimed that of all the women he had known, she had the most intrinsic class.

Hyams has described her in recent years: "Even today, seeing her from a distance on a city street, striding easily with head thrown back, you would know why she interested Bogart from the day they met. She was no ordinary girl then, just as today she is no ordinary woman. In fact, she is an extraordinary one."

Hyams added: "Many things would change in the decades since Bogart's death, but even today, seen close-up and without make-up, her face has not lost its distinctive line. But it is her eyes that rivet you. Feline, clear, gray, unwavering—penetrating, studying and sometimes mocking, making no attempt to hide the fact that they are evaluating, judging and assessing you. And if you are found wanting or ordinary or dull, they will shut you off."

Many film historians and journalists over the years, including myself, have commented that, at 19, she smashed through to movie fame on sheer impact and chemistry—both youthful elements. But today, in her seventh decade, Bacall has presence, charisma, the force and authority that only the richest life experience can convey.

Hyams among others noted that despite her splendid professionalism, her strong moral sense, her inherent decency and right-mindedness, her ready acceptance of responsibility as actress, wife, and mother—much of which she owed to Bogart's early influence—"not all that rubbed off [from Bogart] is pleasant in a woman. The hard-boiled, sardonic attitude that was part of his character and hers, when she was young, is not always charming in an older woman. But it is as much a part of her as it was a part of him because, in the final analysis, they were mirror images of each other."

But the oddest, most miraculous thing of all is that as of 1986, Lauren Bacall, once a 19-year-old screen neophyte who stood in such awe of Bogart's circa-1944 screen magnitude and force of person-ality, is herself a dominating legend of both screen and theatre, a Great Star who exemplifies "The American Experience of the Upward-Mobile" per-haps more pointedly *and* poignantly than any other....

Bacall has always had a good understanding of herself and others. In her autobiography she wrote: "Even after the success of *Applause* (1970), I still had to fight my past life. Whatever people have made of me in their heads—both from my movie career and from my marriage to Bogie—is an obstacle to *now*. They want their memories and fantasies kept in-tact—they're not interested in the person I am."

Of her personal failures with Robards, Cariou, Guardino—and reportedly even the great Adlai Stevenson himself, whom she met during one of her political phases—she has written philosophically.

Friends say that Bacall feels that men require

In Chicago, 1945.

their own individuality and identity, and that they don't want to be tagged in the public mind as "Mr. Whoever." She also has opined that she has found few men who are inwardly secure enough to accept her as she is, without regarding her as a threat, of some kind, to their "masculine self-image" —a complicated term that covers a lot of psychological territory.

Bacall seems to feel it is of cardinal importance that she be accepted as what she is, as of 1986, without regard to the Bacall, either of Reality or Legend, of 1944, 1954, 1964 or whenever, and that in any conceivable intimate relationship she would have to be loved and wanted for herself, alone. "A tall order for a woman of nearly 62, but that is what she wants," one Bacall-watcher has stated.

It has been written of Lauren Bacall that, as was true of Joan Crawford, her youthful idol Bette Davis, and other hardy distaff luminaries, if she were suddenly to find herself confronted with a situation where everything went her way personally and careerwise, she might become bewildered by having nothing to struggle over.

Be that as it may, the lady is a Survivor Transcendent, indeed.

Even for goddesses of her unique persuasion, there has to be a beginning somewhere. Lauren Bacall was born Betty Joan Perske on September 16, 1924—in New York, naturally. Her father, one William Perske, was a salesman. He was of Alsatian origin. Her mother, who came from Rumanian-Jewish stock, was born Natalie Weinstein. In 1931, when Betty was six, her parents were divorced.

After the divorce she saw very little of her father, who seems to have been an unstable man who had trouble finding himself. He was also an eccentric "Indian-giver," who once gave Betty a watch, then asked for it back. He disappeared completely from her life for years, then tried to resume with her when she became famous. This she resented—and told him so.

"Bacal" was the Rumanian equivalent of "Weinstein," and "Bacal" (with one l) was the name that Natalie adopted for herself and Betty after the divorce. A strong-willed woman who believed in facing up to life, Natalie Bacal progressed in the business world, winding up as a secretary. She persuaded her two prosperous brothers to finance Betty at a private boarding school, Highland Manor, in Tarrytown, New York. After Highland Manor, Betty matriculated at Manhattan's Julia Richman High School.

Soon Betty Bacal (she added another l after she went on the stage) was taking ballet lessons, and at first considered a dancing career. Even at 15, in 1939, her excellent facial bone-structure and penetrating gray eyes were attracting attention. Her uncles pulled some strings for her in the New York garment district, and soon she was modelling.

She graduated from Julia Richman High School in 1940, when not quite 16, then went on to the American Academy of Dramatic Arts. Outside of classes, she continued to model for fashion designers, helped publisher Leo Shull peddle his show-biz weekly on the streets around Broadway, and proved so striking in appearance and poised in comportment as an usherette at the St. James Theatre that the famed drama critic George Jean Nathan took personal note of her and described her in a column.

Betty's mother had drilled into her the apothegm that Persistence Wins the Day, and soon she was pestering George S. Kaufman and other Broadway "influentials" into giving her work in plays. On March 16, 1942, still only 17, she showed up in her Broadway advent as a walk-on throughout the action of *January 2 by 4,* a racy and garish play about a

1920s-era Greenwich Village speakeasy and its denizens. *January* got a wintry critical and public reception befitting its name, and ran only briefly. She later told a reporter that even though she didn't get to speak a single word, she found it exciting just walking around in front of all those people; it was also thrilling to know that she had had a "Broadway Baptism," however humbly.

An editor from *Harper's Bazaar* spotted Bacall in the cast, took note of her willowy poise and fine figure, and soon she was appearing in that magazine. Here her prior modelling experience stood her in good stead. Next Bacall (as her name was by then spelled) wheedled her way into another Broadway-bound play, *Franklin Street.* Due to hit New York the Fall of 1942, it closed in Washington, to her great disappointment.

It was back to modelling again, but this time she got a major break. Slim Hawks, wife of the famed director Howard Hawks, saw her on a *Harper's Bazaar* cover in the New Year 1943 (she was 18) and brought the picture to Hawk's attention.

Hawks was working on a screen version of Ernest Hemingway's 1937 novel, *To Have and Have Not* (see section on that film) and he was looking for a fresh, distinctive new face to play opposite its projected star, Humphrey Bogart.

Once arrived in Hollywood and presented to Hawks for inspection, Bacall impressed him as striking and individual in looks but rather rudimentary in acting skills, and he promptly began training her. She signed a seven-year contract at only $250 a week.

She had an odd but arresting habit of lowering her chin toward her chest and peering up intently at a man, and the sharp Warners people realized that this translated, especially via the camera, into a super-sexy come-on and dubbed it The Look—a label that stuck.

Two great entertainers: Bacall and
President Harry F. Truman.

Bogart was impressed with her on sight. "I saw that test, and we're going to have fun together," he told her. It was the prophecy of the century. With the writers building up her role along Dietrich-Mae West man-eater lines, and Hawks showcasing her to maximum advantage, it was apparent that she was going to be a sensation in her first picture.

Bogart, who was weathering domestic traumas with his volatile, alcoholic third wife, actress Mayo Methot, at first did not feel he was in any position to court this strange girl to whom he had become so attracted, but when it became evident that his passion was returned, he and Bacall began a tortuous courtship that resulted in his hard-won divorce from Methot and marriage on May 21, 1945, to the 20-year-old Bacall.

Meanwhile the picture got released. Coverage of all Bacall's 23 films is intensive in other sections of this book, but suffice it to say that she won stardom overnight—and in her first appearance on the screen. Soon Walter Winchell was writing lengthy columns about her, and dubbed her "Bacall of the Wild."

Typical of the critical reaction to the newly-named *Lauren* Bacall was the review of the not-easily-impressed James Agee, one of the most eminent film critics of his time. "Lauren Bacall," he wrote, "has cinema personality to burn…she has a javelin-like vitality, a born dancer's eloquence of movement, a fierce female shrewdness, and a special sweet-sourness. With these faculties, plus a stone-crushing self-confidence and a trombone voice, she manages to get across the toughest girl…Hollywood has dreamed of in a long, long while."

The sexy twinkle of the aforementioned "look" was a constant subject of journalistic analysis all through 1944-45. Takeoffs and paraphrasings of such *To Have and Have Not* lines as "It's better when you help" (when Bogart kisses her) and "If you want anything, all you have to do is whistle" (her kinetically performed come-on) were epidemic all over the country and among the soldiers, sailors, and marines of the war period.

Bacall and Bogart, in New York for the premiere, were mobbed by fans. A mightily impressed Jack Warner bought her full contract from Howard Hawks. She and Bogart were rushed into a new film, *The Big Sleep,* and appeared in a gag shot in yet another film, *Two Guys from Milwaukee.* The screenwriters burned the midnight oil thinking up sexy, provocative lines and innuendoed situations for her that barely passed muster with the Production Code bluenoses.

To Have and Have Not itself, outside of the Bacall-Bogart chemistry and naughty dalliances, did not amount to much. "Slow, tired stuff about Vichy-Free French intrigue, and doesn't even follow the original novel closely," pretty much summed up much of the critical reaction. But the "Bogie–Baby" combine was hot stuff at the box-office.

Then Bacall's career ran into trouble. *The Big Sleep* in which, again under Howard Hawks' careful guidance, she appeared to advantage, was not released for a year and a half for reasons that are still obscure, and instead she was cast with Charles Boyer, under an unsympathetic and aloof director, Herman Shumlin, in *Confidential Agent.* Boyer, whose great talent and authority overawed her, kept his own counsel, and without Hawks to guide her, she floundered badly. She recalled in later years how her inexperience had undone her, and how Shumlin had refused to give her even the most rudimentary guidance.

When *Confidential Agent* was released in 1945's Thanksgiving season, the critics did a cruel reverse on her, many of them publicly declaring that they

The wedding picture.

The bride cuts the cake. Novelist Louis Bromfield with Bogart.

had overrated her acting talents. Boyer and the picture fared decently enough, but the adjectives most frequently employed for Bacall in it were "wooden," "limited to one or two expressions," "stilted," "self-conscious," "zombiesque," and "Jenny One-noteish."

She did recover much of the lost ground with the critics in the next year, when *The Big Sleep* was finally released. "Ah, here's the Bacall we know and love" was typical of the reviewer reaction, with few realizing that *The Big Sleep* had been photographed *before Confidential Agent*—an irony that Bacall and Bogart ruefully noted.

After that, however, Bacall's career settled into a rut. Her marriage was doing famously, and while she was happy being Bogart's wife, she was still ambitious for her career, and began to run up a record for suspensions when she refused one weak picture after another. She appeared with Bogart in two pictures in 1947-48, *Dark Passage,* in which he was an ex-convict out to prove his innocence of a murder with Bacall's aid (the weakest of the films they made togther), and *Key Largo,* a film version of the 1939 Broadway play that had starred Paul Muni, in which Bogart, a war veteran who has become disillusioned with fighting, recovers his manhood in combating a vicious gangster in a hotel on a Florida key.

Surrounded in this by such good actors as Edward G. Robinson, Lionel Barrymore, and Claire Trevor (who won a supporting Oscar for her role), Bacall was highly creditable, if low-keyed, as the hotel owner's daughter who comes to respect, then love, Bogart. In both these films, however, the saucy, piquant, mannishly-aggressive Bacall manner that had won her initial fame was not to be seen. Instead audiences were treated to a quietly confident actress who underplayed her scenes with professionalism but hardly shot off sparks.

Meanwhile, Jack Warner, who had suspended her a dozen times for refusing to do blah pictures like *Storm Warning,* began to lose interest in her, and after two more pictures, *Young Man with a Horn,* with Kirk Douglas, and *Bright Leaf,* with Gary Cooper, she bought out her Warner contract and departed.

The first of these two 1950 pictures, the one with her old friend of New York days, Kirk Douglas, proved to be one of her best performances, however. In *Young Man With a Horn,* as a perverse, restless, envious girl with distinct Lesbian tendencies who proves destructive to herself and those around her, she demonstrated yet again that the arresting personality she had displayed in the Hawks films was no flash in the pan. She herself thinks little of *YMWAH,* but I have always held her performance in this in high esteem, and think it her all-time best on the screen.

The second film, *Bright Leaf,* displayed her attractively as a good-bad girl who loves Gary Cooper but loses him to Patricia Neal—for a time. She doesn't seem to have worked well with Michael Curtiz, however, whom she characterized as a bully, a boor, and a putdown artist.

Meanwhile, she was giving her all to the domestic front, with her first son arriving in 1949, and her

A still from *The Big Sleep*.

Betty tried to make her feel at ease. Bacall was now almost 30, the woman had replaced the girl, and the poised, still sleek and attractive performer who had been married eight years by then, and was mother of two, was hailed by Alton Cook in the *New York World-Telegram & Sun*'s review of *How to Marry a Millionaire* with these words:

"First honors in spreading mirth go to Miss Bacall. The most intelligent and predatory of the trio, she takes complete control of every scene with her acid delivery of viciously witty lines."

The Bogarts began entertaining at their handsome new Holmby Hills home, and were soon among Hollywood's most popular couples. Soon she found herself Den Mother of what came to be known as the Holmby Hills Rat Pack, one of whose leading members was Frank Sinatra. As a duo they were much imitated, with Bacall's deep, sexy voice becoming a new vogue among women, and Bogart's sardonic, iconoclastic opinions and putdowns of puffed-up film moguls and other phonies proving rich sources of amusement among his friends, Hollywood in general, and, in time, the world at large, thanks to much newspaper space given to their offscreen activities.

Friends commented on how the couple were rubbing off on each other, and in some respects, becoming more and more alike. Unfortunately, the roles Bacall did in the 1954-55 period, right after *HTMAM,* did not showcase her distinctive attributes but relegated her, rather, to straight leads where she more or less passively reacted to the goings-on around her.

Woman's World (1954) was an "all-star" picture about corporate aspirers and the women behind them, with archly sardonic Clifton Webb as a top executive looking for a new general manager. In the

daughter, Leslie, in 1952. For a while she was happy with wifehood-motherhood, but soon the old career itch reasserted itself. When she was offered a 20th Century-Fox contract in 1953, she eagerly accepted, and her first picture there, *How to Marry a Millionaire,* demonstrated her sharp comedy timing and shrewd command of racy, biting dialogue as one of the three models in search of a rich husband.

She remembered Betty Grable, one of her two co-stars, as good-hearted and easy-going, but recalls the other, Marilyn Monroe, as shy and insecure, though nice, and has often recounted how she and high-powered cast were Van Heflin, Arlene Dahl, June Allyson, and Cornel Wilde; and Fred MacMurray played a workaholic who has neglected wife Bacall. Despite some effective domestic scenes (if that's the term for them), Bacall found herself lost in the high-powered thespian shuffle around her. Many wondered why she bothered to take the role.

Her two 1955 films, *Blood Alley* and *The Cobweb,* had her again in roles that were much too passive for her temperament. She liked John Wayne very much and enjoyed working with him in *Alley,* but she was merely along for the ride as Big John rescued a gang of hapless anti-Communist refugees. In *The Cobweb,* she found herself awash amidst mental hospital hysterics and indulging in an adulterous affair with a doctor, Richard Widmark. Lillian Gish, as a formidably witchy hospital administator, stole the picture, and Charles Boyer, Gloria Grahame, John Kerr, and kookily-loony Oscar Levant completed yet another all-star cast.

Her next two pictures, *Written on the Wind* (1956) and *Designing Woman* (1957), were made during Humphrey Bogart's harrowing illness (he was to die a slow death, from cancer, on January 14, 1957.) Critics remarked, especially in the case of *Designing Woman,* how professionally she behaved considering the stresses on the home front at the time. But alas, *Written on the Wind* again had her *reacting* to the more colorful mischief-making of her co-stars Robert Stack and Dorothy Malone (who won a Supporting Actress 1956 Oscar for her witchy playgirl). As the hapless wife of deranged oil heir Stack who comes to love his more stable friend, Rock Hudson, she simply languished along, in a passive style entirely unsuited to her true temperament and abilities.

Designing Woman, released some months after

her husband's death in 1957, put her sparkling comedy talents on display opposite Gregory Peck in a picture Spencer Tracy and Katharine Kepburn could have made their own ten years before. She is a fashion designer, he a sports writer, and you take it from there. But while Bacall demonstrated that in her own style she could make something out of a Hepburn role, Peck proved yet again that he was Hollywood's most miscast male star. In a role that cried out for Tracy's shrewd, knowing ministrations and sharp comic timing, he fell flat. "Much too earnest for light comedy," was one critic's verdict on him.

Love.

The Bogarts at home
with their dog, Boxer.

Holiday sailing.

In full regalia for the New York
opening of *The Desperate Hours*.

Bacall, young Stephen Bogart and
Bogart.

The family at home with Boxer.

Bogie admires his Baby. Note Liz Taylor in background.

With the family dogs, 1955.

With Bogart on a radio broadcast.

28

Showing the gams while on her travels, circa 1945.

Clowning with Bogie.

With Bogart, Hepburn, John Huston and African official during filming of *The African Queen,* 1951.

Bacall in her autobiography has described the impact of Bogart's death upon her attitude toward life. Sunk in a deep depression for months after his death, devoted only to the children, she wasn't sure what to do about the future. She wrote of this time: "I didn't have a clue what I was doing. I got up in the morning, talked on the telephone, ate meals, saw friends at home, played with the children—did what had to be done. I was breathing, but there was no life in me. I couldn't think of the future, I could only think about the man I had lost—the man who'd given me everything, taught me about people and living, with whom I had found my way of life. How could I continue alone? How would I fill the days? To what end? He had taken so much with him."

Frank Sinatra had proven very much a comfort during the harrowing final months of Bogart's life, and soon Bacall found herself involved in a romance with him, a romance so serious (at least on her part) that she wanted to marry him. A mutual friend of both has recalled, though, that "while Bogie was a serious, stable man who wanted his home, his career, and one main woman, Frank was more a ring-a-ding type who craved romantic adventurism—and he could be thoroughly unreliable when it came to love."

Enjoying night-club life: Bogart, Mary Livingston and Danny Kaye.

At the time of her marriage to Bogart.

With Bogart contemplating boat model.

Bacall and Bogart lead a delegation of Hollywood luminaries for the morning session of the House Un-American Activities Committee on communism in Hollywood. Behind the stars are Danny Kaye, June Havoc, Paul Henreid, Richard Conte and Ring Lardner, Jr.

At the NY premiere of *How to Marry a Millionaire,* Bacall, Bogart and Marilyn Monroe.

Result: Bacall couldn't figure out where she stood in the Sinatra scheme of things. Then, when Sinatra heard a report that Bacall had publicly stated that marriage was in their future, he dropped her precipitately.

There have been numerous reports, opinions, pronouncements and alleged "inside information" about the true cause or causes of the Bacall-Sinatra bust-up. Basically, it appears that Sinatra, while fancying the role of good samaritan to a friend's distraught widow, tended to shy off when serious romance—let alone marriage—emerged on the horizon. "At that point Frank just wasn't ready for marriage," a friend has said. "He had already been twice-burned; he was concerned about his children, troubled about his first wife, Nancy, and the guilts associated with her, and his Catholic conscience was acting up. Quick romances yes, samaritan to ladies in assorted forms of distress, okay—but marriage, no, not at that point in time."

Over the years, Bacall's feelings about, and memories of, Sinatra proved bewilderingly inconsistent; in 1981 she was panning him to Barbara Walters on TV; in 1985 she was speaking of him with mellow off-handedness to the London press.

During the 1957-59 period, she grew increasingly fed-up with what she considered to be Hollywood's superficial, bitchy, and unfeeling social scene. She also realized, with shocked sorrow, that friends she had had in common with Bogart during his lifetime tended to think of themselves as *his* pals, not hers, and dropped her, or so it seemed to her.

Nor was her morale improved by a weak, sentimental little picture she did for a 1958 release, *The Gift of Love*. In this she was reunited with her *Written on the Wind* co-star Robert Stack, and while their personal association was a pleasant one, she realized—too late—that she had gotten herself into

a soggily sentimental mess about a dying wife who adopts a child as a "gift of love" for her about-to-be-widowered husband. It became apparent to her, also too late, that she was being "used" by cynical Hollywood higher-ups who doubtless felt that the film's plot, with its unmistakable evocations of her recent bereavement, would appeal to handkerchief-wielding housewives. The picture was not a particular success.

But liberation was just around the corner. Bacall went abroad, seeking new emotional as well as geographical horizons, and in 1959, in India, Spain, and London, she shot a fine picture called *Flame Over India (Northwest Frontier* in England). In this she gave a strong, delightfully magnetic and forth-right characterization as an intrepid governess circa 1900 who helps British Army officer Kenneth More rescue a young Indian prince from rebels. She found the atmosphere in India enthrallingly novel and invigorating, and hugely enjoyed shaping her role (this picture contains my second-favorite Bacall performance). Later that year she went back to America in a new mood of emotional euphoria and spiritual independence.

It was late in 1959 that she realized, at long last, that she was a grown woman of 35 with deep and strong inner resources, fully capable of standing and prospering on her own as careerist and mother to her two children, and if Mr. Right the Second showed up, great! If he didn't, she'd get along quite nicely, thank you.

The year 1959 held yet another wonderful bonus for her. She accepted an offer to co-star with Sidney Chaplin on Broadway in *Goodbye Charlie*. Play-wright George Axelrod, a longtime admirer of Bacall's masculine-feminine wry forthrightness, had written the play expressly to her measure. As Charlie, a man-about-town who dies and returns, to

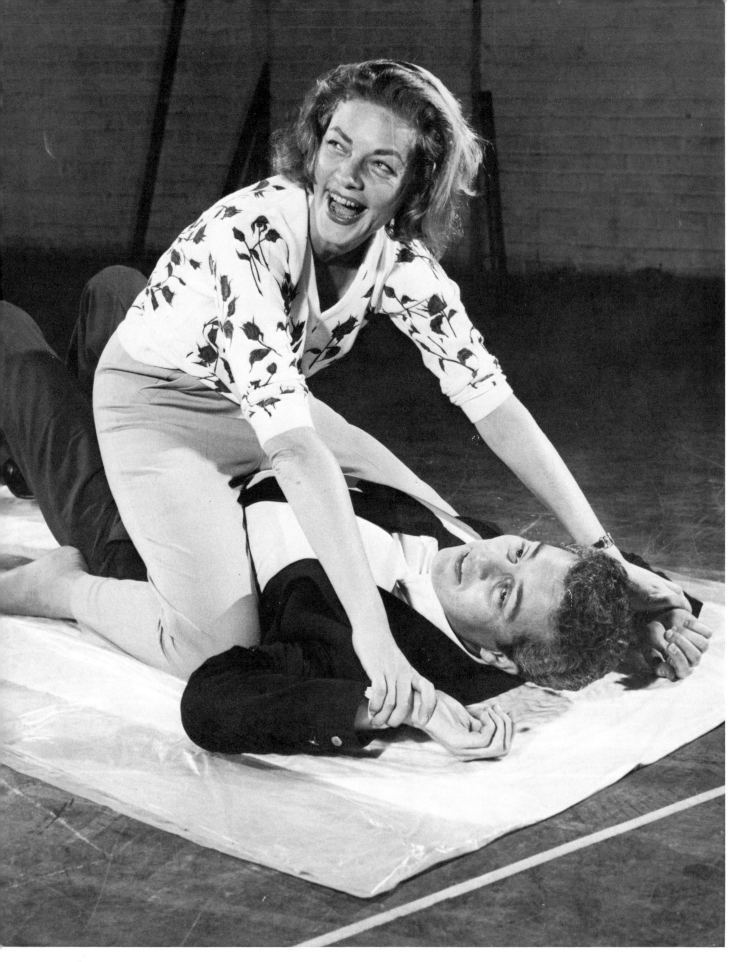

Rehearsing with Sydney Chaplin for the George
Axelrod comedy, *Goodbye Charlie,* in October 1959

Between shots of CBS-TV's *Blithe Spirit* (1956).

Mid 1960s

With Jason Robards, Jr., and their
son, on location, mid 1960s

With Christopher Plummer at the world premiere
of the film *Spartacus,* in New York, October 6, 1960

learn—as a woman—how painful mistreatment by men can be, Bacall proved to be delightfully in her element, won rave reviews, and to her amazement found herself in short order the toast of Broadway, and getting the respectful and admiring accolades that Hollywood had always denied her—at least on *that* level. The prospect of a major career in the theatre loomed up for her; it was a hope that over the years was to be richly fulfilled.

Typical of the reviews for *Goodbye Charlie* was that of the highly-esteemed *New York Times* critic Brooks Atkinson, who wrote: "Miss Bacall gives a good, slam-bang performance—broad and subtle by turns, full of horseplay and guile. If this is the kind of part she wants to play, she can take satisfaction in realizing that she is playing it as well as anyone could."

In 1960-61, however, Bacall found herself again at loose ends. She had moved to New York by then, to the famed Dakota Apartments at Central Park West and West 72nd Street. She turned down several plays that she found unsuitable. It was about this time that she met Jason Robards, Jr., who, like Bogart before him, was already married; he proceeded to romance her on the side. She was later to insist to various reporters that her reputation as a scavenger of other women's husbands was totally unearned, and that it had happened as a result of accident and bad timing.

Robards' problems with ex-wives, money and drink have already been recounted. Bacall fell in love with him, but it was an unwise choice. They conceived a child together but at first he didn't want to marry her. Finally he changed his mind, and after securing a divorce from his second wife, who took it badly and nicked him for a mint for alimony (he had three kids from his first marriage, whom he was also supporting along with their mother), he tied the knot with Bacall in Mexico on July 4, 1961. The marriage, in trouble from the beginning, limped along for eight years, finally expiring—not with a bang but with the proverbial whimper. For Robards, by 1969, it had become a matter of satiety and growing apathy (besides, he had a new woman by then, whom he later married, bringing his wife-count up to four). For Bacall, it was a matter of baffled defeat and dismal depression. She also worried about the effect on their sensitive and impressionable young son, Sam (Born December 16, 1961, five months after his parents married). Friends pinpointed Robards' then-alcoholism, his money bedevilments with expensive alimony and child-support, and his growing emotional disorientation personally and career tensions professionally as the basic causes of the break-up.

With nothing right for her coming up in the theatre, Bacall had accepted, in 1964, two films that she subsequently found disappointing. In a post-1965 interview, she claimed that parts were not offered her in Hollywood very much during that period, that she felt that part of the trouble was that people thought her out-of-date by movie standards because she was associated with the Bogart period. She felt that Hollywood should be reminded that Bogart had been 25 years her senior and that she was not really in an "in-between" age category.

In the first of the 1964 films, *Shock Treatment,* she played a psychiatrist in a mental institution who is carried away by greed for project-funds and winds up crazier than the patients. She recalled that the presence of her old friend, Roddy McDowall, in the cast was one of her few consolations during the shooting. The film got, on the whole, an indifferent reception. At Christmas Time, 1964, she was seen as the shrewish wife of Henry Fonda in the trashy *Sex and the Single Girl,* which borrowed only the title from the Helen Gurley Brown best-seller, then set out to tell a foolish story, only vaguely prurient, about mistaken identities.

The year 1966 brought her what amounted to almost a cameo appearance in *Harper,* which starred Paul Newman giving only a pale approximation of the Bogartian Bite of *The Big Sleep.* In this he was a private eye investigating a millionaire's murder, and Bacall (cast by the producer as an inside joke, her being the former Mrs. Bogart, former *Big Sleep* co-star, and all that) gives an electrically bitchy performance as the missing man's couldn't-care-less wife. The fact she played a paraplegic only made the vitality of her playing the more arresting in this, but Newman, being no Bogart as before noted, found himself out of his element, and the picture suffered accordingly.

Meanwhile, Bacall found herself in another stage hit, reinforcing her growing conviction that theatre audiences would always accord her the major recognition denied her in films. The year was 1965 and the play this time was *Cactus Flower,* "a prickly cactus that blossoms into a beautiful flower," as one writer commented on the title.

Here she was displayed in a carefully wrought, David Merrick-produced, Abe Burrows-adapted play based on the French original *Fleur de Cactus.* She transforms herself in the play from a drably efficient dentist's nurse into a beautiful, exciting lady when her boss persuades her to pretend to be his wife during one of his many romantic dalliances.

The show was a solid hit, and the critics did nip-ups over Bacall, whom they welcomed back to the theatre after a five-year absence with some of the best reviews of her career. Typical of them was the

With Dolores Del Rio in her dressing room during a performance of *Applause,* 1971.

A candid shot of the couple.

World-Telegram & Sun's: "Not many actresses can be grim and endearing at the same time.... Miss Bacall is both, and she tops off the combination with a straight-faced comic delivery which not only sets her role to sparkling but which makes anyone else in the scene look good."

Bacall stayed with the show for two years. Then, after a rest, she went into the 1970 *Applause,* a musical stage remake of the hit film *All About Eve* (1950), which had starred her early idol, Bette Davis. As Margo Channing, Bacall won over all the critics, and the public along with them, and had another long run, winning a Tony into the bargain. Among the encomiums: "A great star, born for the theatre," "sparkling," "authoritative," "immensely winning," "a joie-de-vivre and charismatic force that only the great musical stars can command."

Bacall had found herself in the peculiarly annoying position of playing stage roles that other actresses would do in the movies. *Goodbye Charlie* had gone to Debbie Reynolds, and *Cactus Flower* to Ingrid Bergman. Bacall had been particularly disappointed in the latter instance, as she had believed she would do the role right up to the last minute. "I hate that woman," she had said of Ingrid Bergman, who beat her out. An amusing story has it that Bergman came to see Bacall in *Applause* and later went backstage to see her. Friends wondered if Bacall would receive her, so Bergman sent in a message via Bacall's maid that the woman she "hated" was outside. Bacall laughed graciously, and invited her in for a cordial meeting.

Now things had gone in reverse, and Bacall was not only reprising Davis's film on the stage in *Applause,* but eleven years later was to remake her other idol Katharine Hepburn's film role, *Woman of the Year,* in another solid, long-running stage-musical hit.

Bacall had always found both Davis and Hepburn gracious and cordial when she met them (on equal terms, as against her idol-worshipping days) in later years, and Davis had even come to see her in *Applause.* (There are conflicting stories as to what Davis thought of it.) Bacall had come to know Katharine Hepburn as a friend when she went on location with her and Humphrey Bogart for the 1951 *African Queen.* Bogart had won his only Oscar for this. Bacall found Hepburn a direct, honest, no-nonsense but deeply kind woman, and was proud to claim her friendship for many years, along with that of Spencer Tracy, whom Bacall described as "larger than life but wonderfully unassuming all the same."

As Bacall shifted her creative attentions more and more to her stage career, her film appearances became fewer and fewer. In the entire decade of the 1970s she did only two films for release. *Murder on the Orient Express* gave her a solid character role in the film version of the famed Agatha Christie thriller as a dissolute former actress suspected of a murder. Ingrid Bergman also appeared in it, winning a Supporting 1974 Oscar (Bacall seemed to find herself regularly in films with actresses who got the Oscar that consistently eluded *her*). Bacall remembers *Murder* chiefly for the fine cast, including John Gielgud, Wendy Hiller, and Albert Finney as Hercule Poirot. "It was such a joy and privilege working with, and associating with, such great people," she later said.

Her other film appearance of the decade was in John Wayne's last film, *The Shootist,* in which she played a prim landlady, starchy and disapproving of the dying gunman, who comes to appreciate, before his demise, his more human qualities. Here she was going strictly against type, and many wondered why she had taken the role. "I always liked Wayne from working with him in *Blood Alley,*" she told inter-

With Harry Guardino in *Woman of the Year,* 1981.

In *Applause.*

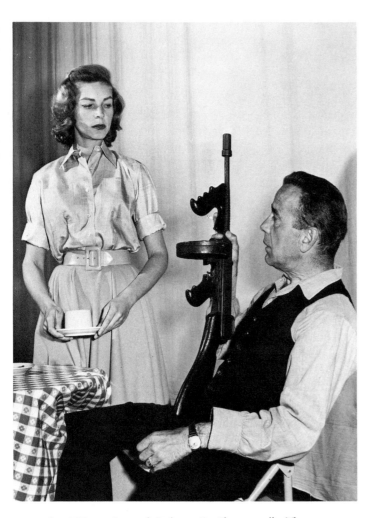

In the TV version of Robert E. Sherwood's *The Petrified Forest*.

viewers, "and I guess I wanted to remind film audiences that I was still around...."

Applause surprised theatre audiences who hadn't realized that Bacall had dancing skills, cultivated from youth. She took singing lessons, and though her celebrated croak became her trademark, she had a definite musical "style" nonetheless. "She gets across the *feel* rather than the *tones* of a song, and that is just as important to the final effect," as one critic put it.

Television has not figured largely in Bacall's scheme of things. She was seen (with Bogart) in the Bette Davis role in the NBC-TV live productions of *The Petrified Forest* in 1955, and in Noel Coward's *Blithe Spirit* (1956), receiving creditable reviews for both. She was in another television production in 1963, *A Dozen Deadly Roses*. She co-starred with John Forsythe on ABC-TV's *Stage 67* in "The Light Fantastic," which covered the history of social dancing in America. She had done some radio at the beginning of her career, and had starred in radio's *Bold Venture* for a twelve-month running. The 1970s found her in such TV fare as the two-part *Rockford Files* as a woman in danger of her life, but it is obvious from her infrequent appearances in the medium that it is not high on her list of priorities.

Bacall has received her share of prizes over the past two decades. She won an American Academy of Dramatic Arts Award for Achievement as far back as 1963, and even copped, in 1967, a Woman of the Year Award from Harvard's Hasty Pudding Club. In 1966 the Women's Division of the Anti-Defamation League of B'nai B'rith hailed her help in "strengthening democracy."

Over the years, always as a registered and declared Democrat, she has interested herself in politics, has been on warm intimate terms with members of the Kennedy family, and supported

With Robert Preston in TV's *A Commercial Break,* 1975.

both Eugene McCarthy and Robert Kennedy. She was a warm and close friend of Adlai Stevenson during Bogart's lifetime, and matters reportedly went to the edge of a flirtation, as her admiration for the two-time Presidential candidate reached the point of the idolatrous. Bogart tended to regard the infatuation with Stevenson, if that's what it was, as just one of her girlish enthusiasms. Bacall has reminisced that Bogart countenanced harmless flirtations—to a point—but warned her that the surest way to destroy marital trust was the indulgence of specifically adulterous conduct. During their marriage she heeded this advice.

There are conflicting reports as to Bacall's specific reaction to the tasteless and vulgarly exploitative book, *Bogie and Me,* by Verita Thompson, a one-time Bogart aide who claims to have been his on-and-off-again mistress during the Bacall-Bogart marriage. According to the book's publicity, "for

fifteen years, Verita Thompson was the friend, confidante and lover of Humphrey Bogart. From 1942 until the day he died in 1957, Verita was at his side, sharing the laughs, the liquor and the bed of this superstar." Many consider it a book in the worst possible taste, a cheap bid for personal publicity from a nobody longing to be a somebody—however belatedly. Bacall's friends have learned never to refer to Thompson or her book in the former Mrs. Bogart's presence. Plainly, though, the sympathy lies all with Bacall in this matter. Some reviewers have opined that Thompson let her romantic imagination run away with her to some extent, but whether smoke indicates fire or not, the Thompson matter is no more than an unsavory footnote to the Bacall-Bogart saga. "Just another hanger-on hungry for a little rub-off attention," is the consensus among Bacall's coterie. And of course, a few bucks help, too.

With Barbara Walters in a TV interview.

Bacall to this day does frequent commercials for all kinds of products, and her rich, smoky voice and commanding manner add spicy amusement to what would otherwise be dullish product-hawking. Norman Norell has made her costumes for the stage, and she continues to wear many of his clothes, and exhibits a sharp fashion sense.

Brooks Atkinson once commented on her "engaging directness" after a personal conversation with her, and Earl Wilson's most-quoted observation on Bacall the Woman is: "She speaks in Capital Letters."

The 1980s found her in two released films. *The Fan* showed her doing what she does best—acting in a stage musical, and "singing", too, of course—and this wild tale of a crazed fan out to "possess" his idol Bacall, even to the point of killing her, is not without its merits, though no Oscar contender for 1981, to be sure. *Health,* shot circa 1979 but not released in New York until 1982, has Bacall as an octogenarian health nut given to suspended animation who seeks election as president of a health organization at a Florida convention. One of Robert Altman's more peculiar conceits, the film has developed a "wacko cult" of sorts, but is one of that eccentric director's lesser efforts.

Woman of the Year, Bacall's second Broadway musical, debuted, as earlier mentioned, in 1981 and won her yet another Antoinette Perry Award. She was altogether delightful in this, and had a long run, later touring the country with it. "Scintillating," "sharp," "exciting," "a lady born for the theatre," "her delicious croak is preferable, so far as this reviewer is concerned, to the finest opera warbling," were among the reactions by the aisle-sitters. As with Len Cariou in *Applause,* Bacall initiated a romance with leading man Harry Guardino, as before noted, but the romance was cold by the time the touring company hit Los Angeles.

During the 1980s she has encouraged the burgeoning acting career of Sam Robards, and takes pleasure in the settled lives of her two older children. Stephen Bogart and his wife have put her in the grandmother category by now—which she takes in stride.

In 1981 she appeared in a candid interview with Barbara Walters, and couldn't resist blasting Frank Sinatra yet again. Despite the fact that she was by then a best-selling authoress via *Lauren Bacall By Myself* (the critics delighted in its forthright candor and no-nonsense writing style, all her own) and had won a Tony for *Woman of The Year,* Bacall still felt herself the underdog in the Sinatra kennel. "I don't see him," she snapped at Walters. "If something ever put us in the same room, one of us is bound to leave and it would probably be him. He has about as much humor as this floor. Have you looked at this floor lately? No humor—not about himself."

She then added: "And if [I and Sinatra] were on the same side of the street, he'd cross over because that is the mentality you are dealing with, so forget it." Then, as a parting shot, she told the stunned Walters that she could have written far worse than she did about Sinatra in her autobiog. "I wish he'd just shut up and sing," she finished.

In 1981 she also had a much-publicized flap with her Dakota neighbor, writer Rex Reed. It was known as "The Battle of the Dakota Bitches." After the 1980 John Lennon murder outside the apartment building, Rex Reed had discussed the building and the celebrities who lived in it, including Bacall, for public consumption, and she let him have it in no uncertain terms for what she felt was an indiscretion and an invasion of his neighbors' privacy. In true "Bitch-Feud" tradition, Reed lashed back at her by panning her performance in *Woman of the Year.*

In mid-1983 Bacall caused a flap on *Entertainment Tonight* by declaring that she "prefers being on the road with a show to being on Broadway because the latter is all about money, commercialism, and she just doesn't approve of the dear old Great White Way in its current state." This courtesy of *N.Y. Daily News* columnist Liz Smith.

Smith let Bacall have it in her column of July 13, 1983. "Well, what is being on the road about? Is it about philanthropy or what? Showbusiness has to be commercial to survive; there is no national endowment for theatre in this country.... A distinguished producer I talked to this week about Bacall's remarks just laughed. 'The road is the most commercial place of all; it needs a superhit or a superstar and that's all there is to it.'"

Smith was not through with Bacall yet. "It is fabulous fun to see Betty Bacall complaining again, just like old times. This lady, who appears to be looking down her nose at commercialism, gets ten percent of the gross of her musical *Woman of the Year,* just as she got ten percent of it when it was a smash on Broadway."

Smith cattily added that the musical was not doing well on tour in Los Angeles, but then sugared the pill with such praise of Bacall as: "[Bacall] is worth every bit of her ten percent. Her professionalism is legend, she never misses a performance and she gives it all she's got every time out." After noting that Bacall had never been in a theatre flop and had always been adored by audiences and critics, Smith continued: "Yet she bitches when the critics rave, when the columnists slather over her, and when the rumors add to her cantankerous but glittering myth. She complained if the producers failed to supply her with two rolls of toilet paper and fresh boxes of kleenex for every performance. I believe it was all in her contract.... It took four limousines to get the star off to the airport when she took off for the L.A.

In Paris, 1975, with French cabaret entertainer Michou, French film star Jean-Pierre Cassel and the remarkable Claudette Colbert.

opening of *Woman of The Year.* For that event the producers supplied her with new scenes, new direction, new choreography, new expensive costumes by Halston, and just about everything else Betty Bacall asked for. But when you have studied at the knee of Frank Sinatra, it's just natural to feel put-upon and complain."

Reportedly Liz Smith's blast aroused the fierce anger of members of the Bacall coterie. "I'd like to see Liz Smith…even *attempt* to approximate the nerve-wracking professionalism and discipline of Betty on stage. Doesn't she realize what night-after-night performing *takes out of* Betty? And if Betty Bacall does ask for special considerations, she eminently warrants and deserves them!" one said.

As is evident, the Bacall Banner is flying high, free, and proud in the decade of the 1980s.

In recent years, Bacall has proven that she has not lost her knack for snappy quotes. Asked if she would ever want to marry again, she replied, "I don't think so, unless the man I was in love with insisted on it. Why get married? I have no intention of having any more children. I've done my bit for the human race. This is the first time in my life I've been entirely free and on my own…. At last I can do what I want to do when I want to do it. A great feeling. Being alone can be real pleasure at any stage in life. I have tremendous energy to devote to myself and my work, and I'm using every minute of it. It's exhilarating. I'm in no hurry to give it up."

On Hollywood: "There are too many things I don't like about Hollywood now. [Such as] the preoccupation with looking young. Whatever happened to growing old gracefully, for God's sake? People have their faces lifted as casually as they have their hair dyed. Sure, I realize I could do with some improvements, but I know I would miss even the bits I don't like if they were to disappear."

After a two-year hiatus from the theatre, in which she occupied herself chiefly with profitable television commercials, Bacall opened in London in July, 1985, in Tennessee Williams' *Sweet Bird of Youth,* with the young American actor Michael Beck as Chance Wayne, and a host of talented English actors making like Southern Gothic types.

Liz Smith this time chose to fall all over Bacall. Her column contained such items as: "Lauren Bacall is on top of the world. The London critics and audiences have gone wild for her in the role of the dissolute film star.... Did Tennessee Williams dream this up years ago with a future Betty in mind? They're dancing in the street in front of the Haymarket Theatre."

Ros Asquith in *The London Observer* wrote: "Lauren Bacall [is] slinky as a lynx, hot as pepper, cool as rain, dry as smoke. There's considerably more to her than staying sexy at 60.... The scenes that sizzle are all Bacall's and if there is a ripple of applause that seems to come from an empty seat somewhere in the gods...then the ghost of Bogie might just be up there somewhere."

New York Times reporter Mel Gussow, reporting from London, wrote: "In *Sweet Bird,* [Bacall] gives a stylish, even a glamorous performance, assiduously scoring comic points. The difficulty is that the character she is playing is not Williams's Alexandra Del Lago, the tormented former movie queen who is grasping for life support. Elegantly coiffed and gowned, Miss Bacall could walk off stage at Theatre Royal, Haymarket, and, without a change of clothes or manner, walk on stage as *Woman of the Year.* In no sense is she ravaged, the single word that sums up Alexandra Del Lago." Discussing the performances of both Bacall and Michael Beck, Gussow continued: "Both stars offer sharp performances of a single dimension, and, in so doing, vitiate the play's

Relaxing after the show.

In *Sweet Bird of Youth* (London, 1985).

primary strength. Unless one believes in their panic—as was the case with Geraldine Page and Paul Newman in the Broadway and film versions—one cannot accept the anguish of the final outcry."

On the other hand, Jack Pitman, reporting from London for *Variety,* tended to agree with the majority of the English critics, writing: "[Bacall] gives a compelling performance as the over-the-hill movie queen who comes up trumps…[she] has the hang of it. She's the right age, has indefinable presence, and she offers a tough interpretation that makes one believe in the character's history, agonies and concerns. Her film queen is still a star-bright personality."

Soon Bacall was opening up to the British press. Under the headline "Stage Star Lauren Lashes Out," Bacall delivered herself of the following:

"I hate liars. And phonies. And people without humor. I can't live without humor…. I'm an actress. I've been in the business 40 years and I'm damned tired of being put in a category by the press. They keep calling me a Hollywood star. I haven't lived in Hollywood for 20 years. I live in New York.

"I resent being regarded as an aging actress. The press considers that after 35, you should cut your throat. Every seven years you've got to shake up your life. I shook up my life when I left pictures and went on the stage. I'm shaking it up again now…and I think I'm wonderful to do it."

She told a London reporter: "I'm not a legend. To be a legend you have to be dead!" (One journalist noted that the Blackglama mink people didn't agree with her when they plunked her into one of their famous "What Becomes a Legend Most" ads.)

Some dame, this Bacall. Her admirers, and they are legion, call her Transcendent Survivor. Her enemies, and they are legion, too, dub her "Biggest Bitch in This or Any Other Town." *I* call her a valiant lady with a whale of a lot of resiliency, a person who has earned her spurs in the tough, cruel game of life and—in her 62nd year—has more than earned the right to come on to the world any damned way she pleases.

With Michael Beck in *Sweet Bird of Youth* (London, 1985).

The Films

TO HAVE AND HAVE NOT

WARNER BROTHERS   1944

Bacall watches a lively discussion between Bogart
and Walter Brennan.

CREDITS

Howard Hawks *(Producer-Director)*; Jules Furthman *(Screenplay)*; William Faulkner *(Associate on Screenplay)*; based on the novel by Ernest Hemingway; Sid Hickox *(Photographer)*; Franz Waxman *(Music)*; Hoagy Carmichael, Johnny Mercer, Stanley Adams *(Songs)*; Charles Novi *(Art Director)*; Casey Roberts *(Set Decorator)*; Perc Westmore *(Makeup)*; Oliver Garretson *(Sound)*; Christian Nyby *(Editor)*.

CAST

Humphrey Bogart *(Harry Morgan)*; Walter Brennan *(Eddie)*; Lauren Bacall *(Marie Browning)*; Dolores Moran *(Helene De Bursac)*; Hoagy Carmichael *(Cricket)*; Walter Molnar *(Paul De Bursac)*; Sheldon Leonard *(Lt. Coyo)*; Marcel Dalio *(Gerard)*; Walter Sande *(Johnson)*); Dan Seymour *(Captain Renard)*; Aldo Nadi *(Bodyguard)*; Paul Marion *(Beauclerc)*; Pat West *(Bartender)*; Eugene Borden *(Quartermaster)*; Elzie Emanuel, Harold Garrison *(Black Urchins)*; Sir Lancelot *(Horatio)*; Major Fred Farrell *(Headwaiter)*; Pedro Regas *(Civilian)*; Adrienne d'Ambricourt, Marguerita Sylva *(Cashiers)*; Edith Wilson *(Black Woman)*.

Opened at the Hollywood Theatre, New York, October 11, 1944. Running time, 100 minutes.

To Have and Have Not has been greatly (and tediously) fussed-over by auteurists and would-be liberals who profess to find in this mishmashed screen version of Ernest Hemingway's 1937 novel a profundity, a multi-dimensional force, and a contrapuntal cleverness that it actually lacks in all the departments so lauded.

By the time producer-director Howard Hawks and screenwriter Jules Furthman got through with it, all essential resemblance to Hemingway, both political and esthetic, was highly diluted and purely coincidental. For one thing, the setting was changed from Key West to Martinique, and the 1937 Chinese smuggled from Cuba became the Free-French leaders smuggled from Vichy, France. Plus other changes too numerous to note. In other words, forget about Hemingway, politics, profound meanings, symbolism, et al., and concentrate instead on the red-hot pairing of Humphrey Bogart and Lauren Bacall.

Certainly she was the hottest thing to hit the screen in some time. Dubbed "The Look" by Warners Publicity because of the provocative glance she could summon when looking a man over, Bacall got the immediate attention of major reviewers, with *Variety* intoning, "She's an arresting personality in whom Warners has what the scouts would call a find. She can slink, brother, and no fooling." Even the hard-to-sell Bosley Crowther of *The New York Times* wrote, "Slumbering of eye and softly reedy along the lines of Veronica Lake, she acts in the quiet way of catnip."

Another writer unburdened himself of the following: "Her husky, underslung voice, which is ideal for the double entendre, makes even her simplest remarks sound like jungle mating cries." But it was James Agee in *The Nation* who really nailed Bacall—and the picture—down: "It gets along on a mere thin excuse for a story, takes its time without trying to brag about its budget or to reel up footage for footage's sake…and concentrates on character and atmosphere rather than plot. The best of the picture has no plot at all, but is a leisurely series of mating duels between Humphrey Bogart at his most

Hoagy Carmichael at the piano.

proficient and the very entertaining, nervy, adolescent new blonde, Lauren Bacall. Whether or not you like the film will depend on whether you like Miss Bacall."

Agee obviously did like her. "I can hardly look at her...without getting caught in a dilemma between a low whistle and a bellylaugh. It has been years since I have seen such amusing pseudo-toughness on the screen."

Hawks and writer Jules Furthman, who had written for Marlene Dietrich, realized that they had in Bacall a Dietrich-Mae West, masculinely-direct,

deep-voiced type who could be built into an explosive new find. Hawks worked with her on deepening her voice even more, and Furthman burned the midnight oil thinking up cockily brazen sex-situations for her, all along double entendre lines to be sure, but obvious enough to any half-way bright cinemaviewers. When it was time for her to sing, they came up with the amazing choice of Andy Williams to dub her voice—the combination of Andy's tones and Bacall's looks-and-gestures made for red-hot listening. A brazen gamble had paid off.

And that dialogue between Bacall and Bogart! "It's

63

Bogart and Bacall becoming involved.

even better when you help," she informs a baffled Bogart after a kissing scene. She makes "anybody got a match?" sound like a super come-on. When Bogart's kisses grow more aggressive, she growls: "I like that, except for the beard. Why don't you shave and we'll try that again." When she sees Bogart sizing-up Dolores Moran's curves, she lets out with: "What are you trying to do, guess her weight?" And of course, there's the famous: "You don't have to do anything or say anything. Maybe just whistle. You know how to whistle, don't you, Steve? You just put your lips together and blow."

I tend to agree with many of the original 1944 critics who considered *To Have and Have Not* a confused attempt to repeat the disparate, hard-to-duplicate, winning-elements of *Casablanca*. It's not good Hemingway (in fact bears scant resemblance to his original), nor is it Hawks in top form. The picture conveys the unmistakable impression that Hawks gave up on plotting and began, halfway through the project, concentrating exclusively on the explosive Bogart-Bacall chemistry, with writer Furthman following dutifully along.

It remains a mystery forty years later as to why the

A reflective Bogart, a wondering Bacall.

film became such an auteurist and liberal-claque cult, since in its plot essentials it makes neither political nor dramatic sense. The critics of 1944 (much berated by the "intellectual" reviewers of subsequent decades) called *THAHN* "an excuse for some good scenes," "a tinny romantic melodrama," "spiritless," "half-hearted," "slight," with *Variety* declaring, "[The film] fails to materialize as any more than average, somewhat measuredly-paced melodrama where exciting action was rightfully anticipated." The review went on to sprinkle its observations with phrases like "too leisurely" and "entirely undistinctive."

The plot, murky and slight and often confused, had Bogart renting out his small cabin cruiser on the island of Martinique. The time is 1940, soon after France has fallen to the Nazis. A De Gaullist, Gerard, wants him to smuggle in an underground leader from France. At first Bogart refuses, as he considers himself apolitical.

Enter Bacall, as Marie Browning, a girl from points all over the compass, and her cynical, off-hand, but red-hot flirtation with Bogart begins.

Walter Brennan intrudes his presence as a boozy pal of Bogart's, and uses up more footage than his character deserves.

Let's see, they all get caught in a raid by the Vichy-dominated police, which pre-empts Bogart's funds; he agrees to help out the De Gaullist to pay Bacall's fare back to the States; he picks up the underground leader; finds that Bacall has not used the ticket he paid for. There is some confused violence, with Brennan held as hostage by the bad guys. Bogart rescues him, turns the villains over to the De Gaullists, and leaves Martinique with Bacall and Brennan.

That is the sum total of the plot so far as any rational viewer can make out, and a confused mess it is, too slow, long-drawn-out, and lacking in action at the very points where action is mandatory. But forget about all that; when it is theatrically revived (as it often is) or telecast, or is pulled out of your videocassette file for a fresh look-see, concentrate on Bogart and Bacall and their lively, sexy scenes together. Those are this film's sole enduring *raison d'être*.

CONFIDENTIAL AGENT

WARNER BROTHERS   1945

Boyer plays while Bacall waxes dreamy and
thoughtful.

CREDITS

Herman Shumlin *(Director)*; Robert Buckner *(Producer)*; Screenplay by Buckner; based on a novel by Graham Greene.

CAST

Charles Boyer *(Denard)*; Lauren Bacall *(Rose Cullen)*; Victor Francen *(Licata)*; Wanda Hendrix *(Else)*; George Coulouris *(Captain Currie)*; Peter Lorre *(Contreras)*; Katina Paxinou *(Mrs. Melendez)*; John Warburton *(Forbes)*; Holmes Herbert *(Lord Benditch)*; Dan Seymour *(Mr. Muckerji)*; Miles Mander *(Brigstock)*; Lawrence Grant *(Lord Fetting)*; Ian Wolfe *(Dr. Bellows)*; George Zucco *(Detective Geddes)*.

Opened at the Strand Theatre, New York, November 2, 1945. Running time, 118 minutes.

Confidential Agent (1945) was made after *The Big Sleep* but released before it. Warners felt that Bacall needed, for her second film in release, exposure opposite a top male star, and Charles Boyer was elected. The film has gained in prestige and critical esteem since it was originally released, when it was generally dismissed as just another anti-fascist cloak-and-dagger melodrama. Charles Boyer never listed *Confidential Agent* as one of his favorite pictures, but actually it features one of his better performances, and he is extremely professional in his projection of a disillusioned and world-weary mood as a middle-aged Spanish Loyalist who comes to London to head off a business deal being engineered by the Fascists in England.

Boyer finds himself up against such unsavory types as Katina Paxinou, who sets herself firmly in her own special niche, in this film, as one of the screen's most arresting and malevolently intense heavies. George Coulouris, George Zucco, and Peter Lorre are also along for the ride, and add their own sinister presences to the proceedings. Of course Boyer foils the heavies and survives in one piece, but the goings-on are grim indeed before he winds things up. Boyer so doubted the potential impact of the film (he had inherited a role originally intended for Paul Muni, then Edward G. Robinson, then Bogart,) that he immediately went into *Cluny Brown* with Jennifer Jones in order to restore the balance against any critical or popular negative-reaction to *Confidential Agent.*

Which brings us to Bacall. The critics clobbered her mercilessly in this, and some of them claimed that her fine initial performance in *To Have and Have Not* must have been a fluke, or was puppeteered by Howard Hawks, so bad was she opposite Boyer. Bacall herself has admitted that her performance was not up to par, but blames the director, Herman Shumlin, who, she claims, gave her no guidance whatsoever as to the nuances or shadings of her role and left her entirely on her own. Shumlin had been a stage director, and *Watch on the Rhine* (1943) had been his only previous film. As Bacall recalls her trials and tribulations with Shumlin: "He would not allow me to see the rushes and gave me none of the help which I so desperately needed. One would have thought—hoped— that someone, somewhere, would have cared whether I conveyed some sense of character I was playing, but there was never a suggestion from Shumlin that I alter my speech, change an inflection,

John Warburton, Bacall, and Boyer seem to be taken aback here.

Bacall doesn't seem to be feeling well. Love scenes too heady?

convey a particular attitude."

At 20, Bacall was professionally insecure indeed, and without Hawks to guide her, she felt truly lost in this. She remembers ironically that the critics did nip-ups of praise when *The Big Sleep* was released the following year—Bacall Is Back Being Her True Stellar Self Again conveys the gist of their comments—and none of them seemed to realize that it had been made *before Confidential Agent,* and held up for release.

It is true that in the picture Bacall is stilted, self-conscious, wooden, non-expressive, somnambulistic. The role as written and directed is colorless to begin with. Though listed as the co-star, she is actually a second-class leading lady here, dragged in to meet, console, conspire with, and reunite with star Boyer when the plot so directed, with Boyer carrying the main plot line and most of the telling scenes.

Bacall remembers Boyer himself as being "a marvelous man, a first-class actor," but describes him as a gentlemanly, reclusive, self-involved man who was himself troubled by less-than-admirable

Boyer looks mysterious and Bacall looks interested.

aspects of the picture while shooting, and was carrying on his own brand of conflict with the cinematically inexperienced yet crassly dictatorial Shumlin. "Shumlin even tried to tell Boyer, the Greatest Screen Lover of Them All, how to play a *love scene!*" Bacall later snorted in disgust. But when they had scenes together, though she was afraid to ask his advice and had to rely on occasional off-hand hints from Bogart when he visited the set (obviously inadequate hints), Bacall found

Bacall is up to something. Does the inspector sense it?

Boyer gently understanding and, within limits, co-operative. Meanwhile she continued furious with Jack Warner, "who had been so careless with me," and with Shumlin. "Much Ego and No Communication," she dubbed him.

Nor did she care for the rather vulgar ad campaign the Warner publicity people dreamed up for the picture when it was released in late 1945, with posters screaming out observations along the lines of: "What happens between Boyer and Bacall in this is Strictly Confidential!" (or words to that effect).

Still, while the film does nothing for Bacall, then or in retrospect, it is a creditable rendition of the Graham Greene novel—thanks more to Boyer's fine acting and a tautly compelling Robert Buckner screenplay than to Shumlin's heavy-handed direction. When asked about it nowadays, Bacall says: *Please*—I'd rather forget *that* one!"

Typical of the reviews of her work in this was that of Howard Barnes in *The New York Herald Tribune*: "Miss Bacall is decorative and intense, but she has a very tiny range of expression or gesture."

TWO GUYS FROM MILWAUKEE

WARNER BROTHERS   1946

CREDITS

David Butler *(Director)*; Alex Gottlieb *(Producer)*; Charles Hoffman and I.A.L. Diamond *(Screenplay)*; Arthur Edeson *(Photographer)*; Frederick Hollander *(Music)*; Leo K. Kuter *(Art Director)*; Stanley Jones *(Sound)*; Jesse Hibbs *(Assistant Director)*; Irene Morra *(Editor)*.

CAST

Humphrey Bogart and Lauren Bacall *(guest appearance as themselves)*; Dennis Morgan *(Prince Henry)*; Joan Leslie *(Connie Reed)*; Jack Carson *(Buzz Williams)*; S. Z. Sakall *(Count Oswald)*; Janis Paige *(Polly)*; Tom D'Andrea *(Happy)*; John Ridgely *(Mike Collins)*; Franklin Pangborn *(Theatre Manager)*; Creighton Hale *(Committee Member)*; Rosemary DeCamp *(Nan)*; Pat McVey *(Johnson)*; Chester Clute *(Mr. Carruthers)*; Monte Blue, Ross Ford *(Technicians)*; Peggy Knudsen *(Juke Box Voice)*; Patti Brady *(Peggy)*.

Opened at the Strand Theatre, New York, July 26, 1946. Running time, 90 minutes.

Charles Hoffman and I.A.L. Diamond dreamed up an original screenplay for Dennis Morgan and Jack Carson, whose engaging but contrasting chemistries seemed to mesh well on screen. This was the first of their "Two Guys" pictures, the second being 1948's *Two Guys from Texas,* in which they were again directed by David Butler. Neither film was any world-beater, being banal and rather foolish in plotting and situations.

However, in the 1946 *Two Guys From Milwaukee,* the screenwriters had a brainstorm: Let's get those newly-married Bogart and Bacall into a guest situation (the term "cameo" hadn't at that time come into general use) and thus give our admittedly so-so little comedy a windup lift. Windup lift it certainly needed, and with the Bogarts in charge of the final scene, that is what it got.

But meanwhile the audience was treated for some 86 minutes or so to a rather foolish story that not even the hardworking Morgan and Carson could redeem. It seems Morgan is a Balkan prince visiting the United States. (Since Wisconsin-born Morgan, né Stanley Morner, was as American as the proverbial apple pie, complete with midwest accent, this kind of casting stretched the credibility of the audience right off the bat.) He vamooses from a New York reception, hell-bent on seeing how Americans really live. It seems His Highness has two overriding ambitions: to rub shoulders with, and get to know, the common man, and to meet Lauren Bacall, who is his big movie crush. He runs up against cab driver Jack Carson, who proceeds to clue him in on American manners, mores, and morals, such as they are.

Well, it seems that in 48 hours, Prince Dennis is scheduled to deliver an intercontinental peptalk to his unruly and unpredictable subjects, who are holding a plebiscite on whether to stay monarchist or go republican. The police are sent out to look for him, locate him, and bring him back so that he will make his address on time. In line with the usual twists in such plots, a live mike, accidentally switched on ahead of schedule, catches a conversation between Carson and Morgan, and so eloquently raffish is Carson's paean to the American way of life that the Balkan subjects proceed to vote for a republic.

Finding himself out of a job, Morgan is offered a post with a Milwaukee brewery, and on the plane for Wisconsin finds himself seated next to none other than his idol, Bacall. But his joy is short-lived when a dour, tough-acting Bogart shows up suddenly to claim his seat next to his wife.

Two Guys from Milwaukee actually represented the second screen appearance of the Bogarts together, as *The Big Sleep,* which had been made a year and a half before, right after *To Have and Have Not,* was released exactly a month after *Two Guys*—which opened July 26, 1946. *Sleep* showed up in New York on August 23.

Two Guys earned only fair-to-middling reviews, and was quickly dismissed and forgotten, with more than one critic commenting that only the Bogie-Baby gag appearance lifted it above the ordinary. Among the most charitable reviews of the picture was that of Thomas Pryor in *The New York Times,* who commented on the "good direction and zestful playing." Most reviewers called it "perfunctorily amusing," "routine," "uninspired," and "eminently forgettable."

Bacall and Bogart went along with the gag because it amused them, and it *did* constitute a trailer of sorts for their own picture coming up imminently.

THE BIG SLEEP

WARNER BROTHERS   1946

Things are heating up, if those looks indicate anything.

Is Bacall figuring out what she can get away with?

Louis Jean Heydt looks threatening, but Bacall and Bogart keep their cool—somewhat.

CREDITS

Howard Hawks *(Producer-Director)*; William Faulkner, Jules Furthman, Leigh Brackett *(Screenplay)*; Based on the novel by Raymond Chandler; Sid Hickox *(Photographer)*; Max Steiner *(Music)*; Carl Jules Weyl *(Art Director)*; Fred M. MacLean *(Set Decorator)*; Robert B. Lee *(Sound)*; Leah Rhodes *(Gowns)*; Robert Vreeland *(Assistant Director)*; E. Roy Davidson, Warren E. Lynch, William McGann *(Special Effects)*; Robert Burks, Willard Van Enger *(Special Effects Associates)*; Christian Nyby *(Editor)*.

CAST

Humphrey Bogart *(Philip Marlowe)*; Lauren Bacall *(Vivien Rutledge)*; John Ridgely *(Eddie Mars)*; Martha Vickers *(Carmen Sternwood)*; Dorothy Malone *(Bookstore Proprietress)*; Peggy Knudsen *(Mrs. Eddie Mars)*; Regis Toomey *(Bernie)*; Charles Waldron *(General Sternwood)*; Charles D. Brown *(Norris)*; Bob Steele *(Casino)*; Elisha Cook, Jr. *(Harry Jones)*; Louis Jean Heydt *(Joe)*; Sonia Darren *(Agnes)*; James Flavin *(Captain Cronjager)*; Thomas Jackson *(Wilde, District Attorney)*; Theodore Von Eltz *(Geiger)*; Joseph Crehan *(Medical Examiner)*; Trevor Bardette *(Art)*; Emmett Vogan *(Ed)*.

Opened at the Strand Theatre, New York, August 23, 1946. Running time, 114 minutes.

The Big Sleep, Bogart and Bacall's second picture together, has been called a cardinal example of the triumph of style over content. For content read plot, which no critic or viewer has figured out to his

In the famed snazzy cap and jazzy checkered suit.

Getting down to brass tacks—or something.

complete satisfaction in all these forty years. Based on a Raymond Chandler novel, and starring Bogart as private eye Philip Marlowe, the story has something to do with Bogart's nabbing a blackmailer whom a wealthy man has accused of peddling nude pictures of his daughter, nympho Martha Vickers. In the course of much wandering, fighting, questioning, quarreling, and killing, Bogart meets up wtih divorcee Bacall, Vickers' sister— and the two take it from there.

William Faulkner, among others, worked on the screenplay, and he and writers Leigh Brackett and Jules Furthman got so confused about the plot ins-and-outs that they at one point had to go to Chandler for an elucidation—and even then, matters storywise still weren't clear.

But to heck with plot, what counted here was Howard Hawks' shrewd direction, the camera's searching eye for sharp, film-noirish characterizations, and a fast pace. What with all the killings, comings, goings, and what-not, nothing made sense, admittedly, but who cared, many a critic admitted,

Bacall knows better than to leave lecherous Bogie alone with unconscious Martha Vickers.

What's on Baby's mind as Bogie lies tied up?

when whatever-it-was purveyed so entertainingly. Many scenes and situations are plunked into the film for their own sake, but individually they are so sharp and pungent that the general effect is to make the audience sit and wait for startling gems of pure, engaging fun.

And then there's the Bogart-Bacall chemistry. And the wicked dialogue that sneaks by the production code (Hollywood's 1946 Mr. Clean) by a hair. When they kiss, Bacall gently growls, "I like that; I'd like more," and when they engage in a conversation that ostensibly is about horses and racetracks, Bacall remarks that her enjoyment depends on "who's in the saddle." Even the most innocent viewers of 1946 got the point. On another occasion she asks him, "What's wrong with me?" and he whips back, "Nothing you can't fix."

Emotionally overwrought sister Vickers (Bacall's sister, that is) messes around coyly with Bogart, who informs her, "I'm cute. There's no one cuter." Later, he switches from sly narcissistic innuendo to leering lustfulness as he watches an unconscious Vickers lying on a bed and Bacall, on to his naughty thoughts, stands guard over her sister and shoots him a look that could annihilate an army tank.

A number of the critics found the film, with its film-noirish atmospherics and clanging confusions, a puzzlement but a fascination. One critic intoned: "I threw up my hands trying to get to the bottom of it, but maybe trying to decipher it, while enjoying the little surprises along the way, is part of the fun." James Agee in *The Nation* wrote: "[The film] is a smoky cocktail shaken together from most of the printable misdemeanors and some that aren't—one of those Raymond Chandler Specials which puts you, along with the cast, into a state of semi-amnesia through which tough action and reaction drum with something of the nonsensical solace of hard rain on a tin roof."

The title, of course, refers to Death. And Death pops up often—indeed with terrifying but never boring repetitiveness—as Bogart, with Bacall popping in and out, wades through an assortment of gangsters, pornographers, sleazes of all types, shapes, sizes and colors. The trail, to make a long and really tangled tale short, leads in time to arch-villain Eddie Mars (John Ridgely) who proves to be the chief malefactor of—well, *that* isn't exactly clear—lots of mischievous murders is the best guess.

It all winds up with Ridgely getting killed, and Bogart and Bacall awaiting the arrival of the police. Even then there is some sexual innuendo, with Bacall more than justifying her new monicker with the press and public, "The Look." Made in late

Forget it, Louis Jean Heydt—those two are unflappable.

1944–early 1945 and not released until the summer of 1946, *The Big Sleep* ranks with *To Have and Have Not* as a top-drawer Bogie-Baby special. Don't let's ask for the moon of clarity and smooth-running story twists; we have here the stars of entertainingly engaging and mesmerically riveting individual situations which somehow add up to sparkling entertainment. One writer said of it, "Howard Hawks brilliantly choreographed the film's numerous killings with awesome inventiveness. Confusing it may have been, but dull it certainly wasn't." And for a cherry on the sundae, count in a wow of a Max Steiner score!

DARK PASSAGE

WARNER BROTHERS   1947

Bacall helps Bogart when he disguises his face via plastic surgery.

CREDITS

Delmer Daves *(Director)*; Jerry Wald *(Producer)*; Based on the novel by David Goodis; Sid Hickox *(Photographer)*; Franz Waxman *(Music)*; Charles H. Clarke *(Art Director)*; William Kuehl *(Set Decorator)*; Perc Westmore *(Makeup)*; Dolph Thomas *(Sound)*; H.D. Koenekamp *(Special Effects)*; David Weisbart *(Editor)*; Bernard Newman *(Wardrobe)*; Dick Mayberry *(Assistant Director)*.

CAST

Humphrey Bogart *(Vincent Parry)*; Lauren Bacall *(Irene Jansen)*; Bruce Bennett *(Bob Rapf)*; Agnes Moorehead *(Madge Rapf)*; Tom D'Andrea *(Taxi Driver)*; Clifton Young *(Baker)*; Douglas Kennedy *(Detective)*; Rory Mallinson *(George Fellsinger)*; Houseley Stevenson *(Dr. Walter Coley)*; Bob Farber, Richard Walsh *(Policemen)*; Tom Fadden *(Waiter)*; John Arledge *(Man)*; Ian MacDonald *(Policeman)*; Ramon Ros *(Waiter)*; Craig Lawrence *(Bartender)*; Lennie Bremen *(Ticket Clerk)*.

Opened at the Strand Theatre, New York, September 5, 1947. Running time, 106 minutes.

Consulting about how to find the true murderer or
murderess.

Dark Passage is generally regarded as the weakest of the four Bogart-Bacall films. Directed by Delmer Daves with what one critic termed "an overabundance of film noir," it sported a rather hokumey plot carried largely by Bogart's assurance and Agnes Moorehead's kookily manic but arresting portrait of a murderess.

Bacall showed a mellowness in her approach and a quiet added assurance, plus a gift for effortless underplaying, that spoke well for her tutelage under Bogart's veteran influence; in other words, his own great talent and seasoned expertise awoke, by association, her own nascent abilities. However, her role tends to be rather colorlessly good-girl-ish here, and this prevents her from registering more dynamically.

"Mr. Bogart is his assured self here," one reviewer wrote, "and Miss Bacall shows that as an actress she is learning and growing, and looks very handsome to boot." But some critics opined that Agnes Moorehead stole the picture, even under the handicap of relatively few scenes.

Among the adjectives employed by critics of 1947 for *Dark Passage* were: "fair-to-middling," "reasonably interesting," "workmanlike" and "gimmicky but respectably presented."

Bacall remembers hugely enjoying the San Francisco location shooting. Cameraman Sid Hickox followed up on a technique well-publicized earlier in the year in Robert Montgomery's Metro-Goldwyn-Mayer picture, *Lady In The Lake,* an adaptation of a Raymond Chandler novel, in which detective Philip Marlowe (Montgomery) appeared (or rather didn't appear) via subjective-camera techniques, while the camera itself, facing the other protagonists, smoked cigarettes, punched people out, etc. In *Lady In The Lake,* Montgomery, seen fleetingly in mirrors, appears full-force only at the close.

A tense moment with Bennett and Moorehead.

Bogart looks at his new face in the mirror, courtesy
of a plastic surgeon.

Warners decided that this was a clever gimmick
indeed, and had Hickox adapt it to *Dark Passage,*
with the diffrence being that Bogart was not seen,
via subjective camera, until forty or so minutes into
the film.

The plot has to do with an escaped convict,
innocent of his wife's murder and determined to
prove his innocence,who hides out in the apartment
of an artist, Bacall, who sympathizes with him
because her father had suffered a similar
misfortune.

Bogart, in desperation, decides to undergo plastic surgery to alter his appearance. (This fitted in
well with the subjective-camera's first 40 minutes in
which he is not seen, so we never know what his
face looked like originally.) A friend who helps him,
Rory Mallinson, is later found murdered.

Bogart remains in Bacall's apartment until his face
is healed; then he sets out to find the person who,
he is certain, has murdered both his wife and his

Will they make it through? The gun should help.

Looking mighty rattled by Moorehead's sinister stare.

friend. He manages to find out, from a petty crook who tracks him to a hotel room intending to blackmail him, that Moorehead's car was seen in the vicinity of the murdered man's apartment.

Bogart, convinced that Moorehead, who was a friend of his late wife's and whose testimony convicted him, is the real murderess. He confronts her at her home, but, after admitting her guilt, Moorehead falls to her death from a window and robs Bogart of his alibi.

Knowing that he cannot find any justice from the law, he flees to South America, where he is joined by Bacall for a "happy ending"—of sorts.

A host of minor characters help *Dark Passage* establish its "noir" atmosphere in depth. Clifton Young is slimy and mean as the blackmailing crook, and his scenes with Bogart have the proper sleazy negativity. Douglas Kennedy is the perfect detective

for this sort of ambience, and Bruce Bennett is odiously suave as the man who—for a time—persuades Bacall he would make decent husband material. As for Moorehead, she would have dominated the film had her footage been longer.

The Bogart-Bacall combine gets little chance to romance, and when they do, the interludes are regrettably short. Their stellar interplay and celebrated chemical blending are sacrificed to the noirish theme, and even at the end, in their South American haven, their tart exchanges and sophisticated badinage, so lavishly offered in their first film, are given short shrift—just enough to titillate and not enough to fulfill audiences who had come to expect this sort of thing from them.

Dark Passage provided the basis for a popular and long-running television series in the sixties—*The Fugitive,* starring the late David Janssen.

KEY LARGO

Bogart regains his will to fight, to Bacall's relief.

CREDITS

John Huston *(Director)*; Jerry Wald *(Producer)*; Richard Brooks and John Huston *(Screenplay)*; Based on the play by Maxwell Anderson; Karl Freund *(Photographer)*; Max Steiner *(Music)*; Leo F. Kuter *(Art Director)*; Song by Howard Dietz and Ralph Rainger; Fred M. Maclean *(Set Decorator)*; Leah Rhodes *(Wardrobe)*; Perc Westmore *(Makeup)*; Dolph Thomas *(Sound)*; William McGann, Robert Burks *(Special Effects)*; Rudi Fehr *(Editor)*.

CAST

Humphrey Bogart *(Frank McCloud)*; Edward G. Robinson *(Johnny Rocco–Howard Brown)*; Lauren Bacall *(Nora Temple)*; Lionel Barrymore *(James Temple)*; Claire Trevor *(Gaye Dawn–Maggie Mooney)*; Thomas Gomez *(Curley)*; John Rodney *(Deputy Clyde Sawyer)*; Marc Lawrence *(Ziggy)*; Dan Seymour *(Angel Garcia)*; Monte Blue *(Sheriff Wade)*; Jay Silverheels, Rodric Redwing *(Osceola Brothers)*; William Haade *(Ralph Freeney)*; Joe P. Smith *(Bus Driver)*; Pat Flaherty, Lute Crockett, John Phillips, Jerry Jerome *(Ziggy's Henchmen)*; Felipa Gomez *(Old Indian Woman)*.

Opened at the Strand Theatre, New York, July 16, 1948. Running time, 101 minutes.

Key Largo is a film that Bacall remembers with pleasure. She enjoyed working with John Huston and the fine cast, which included Bogart, Edward G. Robinson, Lionel Barrymore, and Claire Trevor, who won a Supporting Actress 1948 Oscar for her role as gangster Robinson's pathetic moll who has seen better days.

Bacall tries to get Bogart to remember her war-hero husband's last hours.

Based on a Maxwell Anderson play that had starred Paul Muni, the screenplay is updated to post-World War II and concerns a disillusioned war veteran, Bogart, who has lost faith in fighting as a solution for evil, and who comes to a hotel off the Florida coast, on one of the keys (hence the title), to visit the widow of an army pal, Bacall, and her father, Lionel Barrymore, the establishment's proprietor. There he encounters Robinson, a sinister gang chieftain on the lam, and his henchman. When he

attempts to console the much-put-upon Trevor, he is insulted by Robinson for his pains, and when Robinson's evil nature is highlighted after he frames some Indians for the murder of a sheriff's deputy whom he himself has killed, Bogart recognizes in him the brutal, fascistic, tyrannical, Hitlerian figure who must be countered at all costs.

Bacall and Barrymore, who at first had found themselves disillusioned with what they perceived as Bogart's disinterested timidity, invite him to

Barrymore, Bogart and Bacall discuss his dead war-hero son, shown in picture.

remain with them. Robinson wants to go on to Cuba, and commandeers Bogart to pilot the boat. On board, Bogart eliminates the gang one by one, until he is down to Robinson, who cravenly offers him money in exchange for his life. Bogart scornfully dispatches him, too, then returns to Key Largo and the waiting Bacall.

There was a great deal of pseudo-profound discussion about the anti-fascist, anti-Hitler, anti-tyranny implications in *Key Largo,* much of which seems outdated to 1980s eyes, and simplistic to boot, but the picture puts itself over, largely thanks to John Huston's shrewd eye for characterization and pacing and atmospheric effects, and to the fine acting of Bogart, Claire Trevor (pitiful yet magnetic in her role of the moll who has seen her best days), and, above all, Robinson, who at age 55 showed he had lost none of his sinister command as the gang chieftain. Whether whispering obscenities in a shocked-and-repelled Bacall's ear, or sitting in a tub with hat on and cigar in mouth, looking sinisterly riveting, Robinson takes the picture for his own.

This is not to underrate Trevor's fine performance, so amply deserving of an Oscar, or Bogart's subtle delineation of the disillusioned war vet who reawakens to the fact that fighting for a just cause, with a positive, clear-cut motivation, has intrinsic humanistic rewards.

Bacall looks extremely attractive as lensed by Karl Freund, and underplays touchingly and with more than a little skill her role of a war widow who had lost (until Bogart's heartening advent) any true *raison d'etre* in her life. Lionel Barrymore, in fine theatrical fettle, is touching as the old hotel owner who still believes that good people, working together, can overcome the forces of evil.

Max Steiner helps things along with an evocative, richly-themed score, and Freund's photography

Claire Trevor, Robinson's forlorn moll, finds a friend in Bogart.

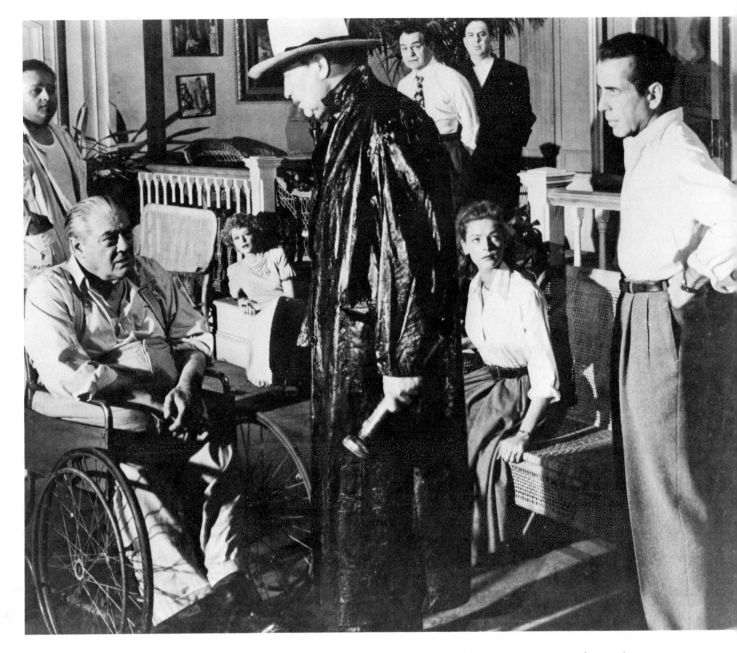

There's trouble afoot for all on Key Largo: Dan Seymour, Lionel Barrymore, Claire Trevor, Monte Blue, Robinson, Thomas Gomez, Bacall and Bogart.

makes the most of the *mise en scène* provided. Richard Brooks wrote the screenplay with Huston, and learned much about directing from watching The Master on set.

Bacall was credited by a number of reviewers with deepening her professional approach, and *she* always credited whatever values were in her performance to Huston's guidance and the stimulating presence of the other fine actors. She even got a fair share of good reviews, including one from *Newsweek*, whose reviewer wrote: "The surprise of *Key Largo* is Miss Bacall, who forgets her curves to play Nora straight and comes off with a forthright, credible characterization."

Bacall is especially good in scenes with Bogart in which she seeks to learn from him about her husband's last hours, and when she observes Bogart's initial reluctance to involve himself in conflicts of any kind, having had enough of these in a war he has come to regard as a Mammoth Exercise in Futility. And her eloquently limned renewal of hope and positivism, as she sees Bogart revert to the fighter-against-injustice he was born to be and remain, is not without its touching aspects. It is easy to see why Bacall always looks back on *Key Largo* as a positive, refreshing experience.

YOUNG MAN WITH A HORN

WARNER BROTHERS   1950

She is tormented by envy of her husband's talent.

Day realizes she is odd woman out in *that* threesome!

CREDITS

Michael Curtiz *(Director)*; Jerry Wald *(Producer)*; Carl Foreman and Edmund H. North *(Screenplay)*; based on the novel by Dorothy Baker; Ted McCord *(Photographer)*; Edward Carrere *(Art Director)*; Ray Heindorf *(Music Director)*; Alan Crosland, Jr. *(Editor)*.

CAST

Kirk Douglas *(Rick Martin)*; Lauren Bacall *(Amy North)*; Doris Day *(Jo Jordan)*; Hoagy Carmichael *(Smoke Willoughby)*; Juano Hernandez *(Art Hazzard)*; Jerome Cowan *(Phil Morrison)*; Mary Beth Hughes *(Margo Martin)*; Nestor Paiva *(Galba)*; Orley Lindgren *(Rick as a boy)*; Alex Gerry *(Dr. Weaver)*; Walter Reed *(Jack Chandler)*.

Opened at Radio City Music Hall, New York, February 9, 1950. Running time, 111 minutes.

Young Man With a Horn contains my favorite Lauren Bacall performance—in fact, I consider it her all-time best. Bacall's complaints about the poor roles Jack Warner assigned her cannot fairly be applied to the character of Amy North, the spoiled, willful and perverse rich girl who marries trumpet-player Kirk Douglas. She bitterly envies her husband's musical talent, feeling she has no abilities of any kind of her own, and almost destroys him before they part. The screenwriters, Carl Foreman and Edmund H. North, really did Bacall a favor here—giving her a role that is well-written, dimensional, tangy—and in some areas ahead of its time. For Messrs. Foreman and North slyly inserted a lesbian

Day and Douglas as relaxed as Bacall will ever let them be.

(Below) Bacall's perversities dumbfound her hapless spouse.

Douglas will regret his initial enthrallment.

angle that was revolutionary for 1950—and how it got by the superprude Production Code people remains a mystery to this day.

Of course, a lot of the censors of that time were not very bright or subtle-minded folk, and when confronted with Bacall in the process of taking up with a young woman she evidently finds more congenial than her husband, they missed the intense nuances and probably assumed that our girl was just looking for a pal's shoulder to cry on. Some pal. The actress assigned the role (little more than a bit) literally devours Bacall with her eyes, and Bacall obviously enjoys the admiration—or, anyway, her character does.

Bacall tries to explain her complex needs.

Bacall is all the more admirable in this part because her attraction to the male sex in private life has never been questioned. But her character, Amy North, is limned in a style any first-class actress could respect. Bitter, frustrated, a non-talent who dilettantes all over the place, a dabbler in all arts and a mistress of none, Amy has a destructive streak. She marries talented trumpeter Douglas feeling subconsciously that some of his talent may rub off on her; when it doesn't, she turns cold and unresponsive, manages to be asleep when he comes home at night and is gone before he wakes, and in one of their quarrels, smashes his record collection. Soon she is off to other pursuits, including the apparently lesbian woman who appears fleetingly.

Douglas's trumpet player, a brilliant musician but rather a naïve type and a poor judge of women, is shattered by the failure of the marriage. "You're sick, Amy," he says to her in bewildered noncomprehension. By 1986 psychological standards, Amy hasn't found herself, and is splashing water on everyone around her while she tries to—but be it 1950 or 1986, as a viewing experience it is highly arresting to watch Bacall get across her character's tormenting complexities. Bacall, oddly, has never thought much of *Young Man With a Horn:* "Unhappily, it was nowhere as good as it should have been" are her exact words. She seems to recall more vividly what a martinet director Mike Curtiz was ("He called actors 'actor-bums,'" she remembers indignantly.) Douglas she liked; they had known each other at the beginnings of their respective careers in New York; she claims he got into movies because she recommended to Hal Wallis that he watch Douglas in a New York play in 1946. "[Douglas and I] worked well together, liked each other, talked over old and new times, and flirted—harmlessly," she later remembered.

New motherhood may have matured her at 24; her work in *Young Man With a Horn* far surpasses anything she had done before, and presages her great work on the stage decades later. Douglas, fresh on the heels of his hit *Champion,* is vital and charismatic in the inimitable Douglas style as a self-destructive trumpet-player who wants to strike that elusive high note and fails—and turns to drink, sliding inexorably downhill despite the loving supportiveness of singer Doris Day, who loves him unrequitedly, and sidekick Hoagy Carmichael.

Good-girl Day has eyes for Douglas, but *his* eyes are for Bacall.

Based on a novel by Dorothy Baker, *YMWAH* had been inspired by the career of Bix Beiderbecke, a jazz-age cornetist who went to the top of his field, then sank into alcoholism and death in 1931 at age 28. Baker didn't model the book precisely on the tragic Beiderbecke's life, but sought to catch the essence of the man. This is one of Douglas's finer performances; he conveys all the passion, inner torment, neurotic perfectionism of a psychologically simple man driven by instinctual demons he does not understand. Day is kindly and tender as the singer, but she is strictly a Jenny-One-Note beside Douglas and Bacall. Hoagy Carmichael, who actually knew Beiderbecke, is effective as the sidekick, and the admirable Black actor Juano Hernandez is affecting as the musician who initially inspires Douglas, and who later goes to seed and dies. Douglas's impassioned playing at Hernandez's funeral is one of the more affecting scenes in the film.

Curtiz kept the pace lively and the situations biting, and music director Ray Heindorf deserves much credit for the apposite musical interpolations. Doris Day shines only when she sings the fine standards she is assigned. But with all due respect to Douglas and his fine playing, it is Lauren Bacall, in her smaller but more telling characterization, that stays in the memory.

BRIGHT LEAF

WARNER BROTHERS   1950

Bacall loves Cooper but will she land him?

Embattled Cooper finds racy Bacall a consolation.

CREDITS

Michael Curtiz *(Director)*; Henry Blanke *(Producer)*; Ranald MacDougall *(Screenplay)*; Based on the novel by Foster Fitz-Simons; Karl Freund *(Photographer)*; Stanley Fleisher *(Art Director)*; Victor Young *(Music)*; Owen Marks *(Editor)*; Ben Bone *(Set Decoration)*; Stanley Jones *(Sound)*; David Gardner *(Second Unit and Montage Director)*.

CAST

Gary Cooper *(Brant Royle)*; Lauren Bacall *(Sonia Kovac)*; Patricia Neal *(Margaret Singleton)*; Jack Carson *(Chris Malley)*; Donald Crisp *(Major Singleton)*; Gladys George *(Rose)*; Jeff Corey *(John Barton)*; Elizabeth Patterson *(Tabitha Jackson)*; Thurston Hall *(Phillips)*; Taylor Holmes *(Calhoun)*; William Walker *(Simon)*; Marietta Canty *(Queenie)*; Charles Meredith *(Pendleton)*.

Opened at the Strand Theatre, New York, June 16, 1950. Running time, 110 minutes.

"Overlong," "loose," "drawn-out" and "routine." These were typical reactions by major critics to *Bright Leaf,* Bacall's 1950 swan song to her original Warners deal. And Bosley Crowther, at the time America's most-read critic, spanked Bacall thus: "Lauren Bacall is torpid and dull." Bacall claimed in her autobiography that she was unhappy with the parts assigned her, that Jack Warner was obtusely unresponsive to her complaints, including requests for meatier roles, and that Mike Curtiz, the director, yelled at her rudely, reducing her to tears, while kowtowing obsequiously to the picture's star, Gary Cooper.

Actually, when viewed over thirty years later, *Bright Leaf* showcases Bacall rather attractively. Karl Freund didn't exactly neglect her lighting, and despite Curtiz's nerve-wracking guidance (or per-

Jack Carson displays the money-making cigarettes.

haps non-guidance), she registers with her particular brand of gleaming sullenness and gets across a passion for Cooper that is restrained yet vital. In a role that could be described as a cross between Belle Watling in *Gone With the Wind* and Ava Gardner's good-bad girl in *Mogambo,* Bacall, freshly beautiful at 25 and a new mother to boot, might have really made something of her role if scenarist Ranald MacDougall had set her up more carefully with apt dialogue and more credible situations.

In *Bright Leaf* Bacall finds herself in a standard triangle with Cooper and Patricia Neal (with whom he was having a red-hot affair at the time offscreen). Neal gives a mannered, often-overwrought, but rather vivid and distinctive performance, much-criticized by reviewers of the time for her "grins," "grimaces," and "grotesque stares," but in retrospect more creditable than was then conceded. Neal's problems—like Bacall's—stemmed from the turgid, over-lengthy script, which was short on character analysis and long on superficial melodramatics and sometimes pointless action.

The plot, laid in the turn-of-the-century South, is one of those rambling affairs featuring Cooper as an underdog who is exiled from his hometown by tobacco tycoon Donald Crisp (who plays in his best authoritative-tyrannical style.) Why the expulsion? Crisp doesn't think poor-white Coop is good enough for his daughter, Neal. Of course, this is the stuff of which get-even plots have been made from Cinematic Time Eternal, and Coop happens upon a revolutionary cigarette-making machine, gets his loving but unrequited good-bad gal Bacall (who has a penny or so put away) to finance it—and soon old enemy Crisp is ruined and Coop reigns triumphant in the tobacco and cigarette-manufacturing fields.

To make a too-long script shorter, Neal marries Cooper to save her father, Crisp commits suicide from the humiliation of it all, and then our hero finds he is nursing a female viper in his bosom, for Neal sets out to ruin *him*. He throws her out, the mansion burns, he leaves town—and good-old-

Bacall plays a watch-and-wait game with her man.

Cooper admires Bacall without loving her—enough.

With Jack Carson.

Carson gives Bacall gas-buggy jitters.

standby Bacall is allowed to feel, ever so subtly, that (in the phrase so popular in that period) she may dare hope.

Mike Curtiz, usually so fast-paced and incisive with material like this, found the period heaviness and MacDougall's script awkwardness too much for him here, and his direction tends toward vagueness and long-windedness. Fine actors like Donald Crisp, Jack Carson, Gladys George, Jeff Corey, Taylor Holmes, and Thurston Hall, try very hard to inject excitement and tension, but the material just isn't there.

Jack Warner, despite Bacall's complaints, probably thought he was giving Bacall a sympathetic, dimensional role as the woman of unconventional mores but generous impulses, and with a more sympathetic director, a tighter, better-rounded script, and more care as to close-ups and lighting nuances

Bacall gets businesslike with the men.

(Freund did well, but in Bacall's case, not well enough), Bacall might have had a forward-propelling film here. But the over-all result was negative.

The aforementioned red-hot love affair between the married Cooper and Miss Neal, which had caught flame two years before during the making of *The Fountainhead,* was in full-swing in 1950, which probably accounts for the greater tension in scenes between them than between Cooper and Bacall—which was not Bacall's fault. Victor Young was not the man needed for *this* opus; his soft, relatively-unassertive style of music-making kept the doings relatively low-key when emotions were set to be highlighted. Max Steiner was needed here as never before; his melodious, operatic hyper-emotionalism might have deluded 1950 audiences into believing that there was more to *Bright Leaf* than met the eye. Too bad.

HOW TO MARRY A MILLIONAIRE

20TH CENTURY-FOX   1953

CREDITS

Jean Negulesco *(Director)*; Nunnally Johnson *(Producer)*; Nunnally Johnson *(Screenplay)*; Based on plays by Zoe Akins and Dale Eunson and Katherine Albert; Joe MacDonald *(Photographer)*; Alfred Newman *(Music)*; Cyril Mockridge *(Incidental Music)*; Louis Loeffler *(Editor)*; CinemaScope and Technicolor.

CAST

Lauren Bacall *(Schatze Page)*; Marilyn Monroe *(Pola Debevoise)*; Betty Grable *(Loco Dempsey)*; William Powell *(J.D. Hanley)*; Cameron Mitchell *(Tom Brookman)*; Fred Clark *(Waldo Brewster)*; Rory Calhoun *(Eben)*; Alex D'Arcy *(J. Stewart Merrill)*; David Wayne *(Freddie Denmark)*.

Opened at Loew's State and Globe Theatres, New York, November 10, 1953. Running time, 95 minutes.

How to Marry a Millionaire (1953) was the second 20th Century-Fox film to be made in the CinemaScope process, the first being *The Robe*. It was one of several remakes of a 1932 film starring Ina Claire, Madge Evans, and Joan Blondell, called *The Greeks Had a Word for Them* (later retitled *Three Broadway Girls*). The story, then and later, dealt with three women who join forces and pool wits—the aim being to land rich spouses. Lowell Sherman had made a sparkling film of it in 1932, and the director of 1953, Jean Negulesco, backed up by Nunnally Johnson's production touch, turned it into a bland but pleasing comedy.

Bacall finds the ways of love confusing.

Grable, Bacall, Monroe, three models-on-the-make.

111

At first, gold-digging Bacall thinks rich-old-man Powell is the answer.

Bacall digs those jewels.

Monroe's cynicisms amuse pals Grable and Bacall.

Bacall has recalled that George Cukor first suggested the film to her, and felt it contained a part that would be just up her alley, to inaugurate her new 20th-Fox one-film-a-year-deal. She had by then been absent from the screen for three years. Nunnally Johnson, in addition to producing, wrote the screenplay. He told Bacall, according to her account, that he had never seen her play comedy, and would she make a test? Bogart advised her to trust Johnson's judgment and forget her pride, and she made the test and won the part. She remembers the new and unfamiliar CinemaScope process thus: "As

[it] was a new experiment for everyone, it was difficult. One had to keep the actors moving and not too close together, as the screen was long and narrow. You shot longer scenes in CinemaScope, five or six pages without a stop, and I liked that—it felt closer to the stage and better for me."

Bacall cold-shoulders Mitchell, not knowing he's rich.

The lady surveys her admirer Percy Helton.

Bacall was kind to her co-stars in retrospect. "Betty Grable was a funny, outgoing woman, totally professional and easy." On Marilyn Monroe: "She was frightened, insecure, trusted only her coach and was always late. During our scenes she'd look at my forehead instead of my eyes." Bacall also recalled that Monroe always looked toward her coach at the end of a take, and if she got a headshake in return, she would always insist on *another* take. This meant a dozen or more takes, and Bacall found she'd have to be good in all of them, as no one knew which would be used. "Not easy—often irritating," as she summed it up. But she felt that Monroe had no meanness in her, no bitchery, and was merely fearfully self-involved. Bacall remembers that she and Grable tried as hard as possible to make it easy for Monroe, and that she felt Monroe wistfully envied her own relative emotional security. "Sad, but nice," was her summation of Monroe.

The plot of *How to Marry a Millionaire* had the girls pretending affluence and renting a snazzy Manhattan penthouse. Grable finds herself seduced by married Fred Clark and winds up in a mountain cabin with him. Here she meets forest ranger Rory Calhoun, who eventually wins her. Monroe gets involved with David Wayne, whom she meets accidentally on a plane. Wayne turns out to be her landlord, who is having tax troubles with the IRS. Bacall meets a wealthy tycoon, William Powell, whom she decides to marry for his money.

Then there's the ostensibly broke young man, Cameron Mitchell, to whom Bacall is attracted but whom she rules out because she thinks him poor. Later, on the verge of marrying Powell, she realizes it is Mitchell she wants more than Money, then to her surprise finds out that he's filthy rich. As for Monroe and Grable, they pair off with Wayne and Calhoun respectively.

It's time for a wedding—to the wrong man.

115

Affable Powell charms Bacall. His money helps.

Negulesco directs briskly if superficially, and the pace is smart and fast. Bacall's personal opinion of the film— "funny, witty, even touching" —was shared by most of the film critics of 1953 who found *HTMAM* no world-beater or Academy Award contender but nonetheless a very pleasant, enjoyable experience—with all the stars in top form. It was remarked how well the Bacall-Monroe-Grable chemistry meshed—the on-screen "chemistry" doubtless enhanced by the exceptional compatibility and cooperative spirit among the three. Those who hoped to see a "bitch-feud," three-way-style, erupt on the set were disappointed.

William Powell was singled out for critical praise, as even at age 61 he expertly projected the jaunty dignity and comic timing that had so characterized his prime. As the understanding older man, he played against Bacall with expert insouciance. Wayne, Mitchell and Calhoun supported the stars ably.

Joe MacDonald's technicolor photography flattered all the girls, and Alfred Newman's musical direction displayed that genius in one of his charming, lighter-hearted moods. He even conducted the 20th Century-Fox orchestra for a rendition of one of his original compositions, "Street Scene." Among the critical adjectives tendered *HTMAM*: "dandy," "terrific," "wryly amusing," and "champagne-bubbly."

Otis L. Guernsey, Jr., in *The New York Herald-Tribune*, said of Bacall in *HTMAM*: "[She is] tall and commanding, the brains of the outfit. The script gives her all the sharper sarcasms and she handles them smartly."

She's about to find out that her young admirer is
loaded.

Monroe seems thunderstruck by Bacall's rich admirer Powell.

WOMAN'S WORLD

20TH CENTURY-FOX   1954

CREDITS

Jean Negulesco *(Director)*; Charles Brackett *(Producer)*; Claude Binyon, Mary Loos, and Richard Sale *(Screeplay)*; from a story by Mona Williams; Joe MacDonald *(Photographer)*; Cyril Mockridge *(Music)*; Lionel Newman *(Musical Direction)*; Technicolor and CinemaScope.

CAST

Clifton Webb *(Gifford)*; June Allyson *(Katie)*; Van Heflin *(Jerry)*; Lauren Bacall *(Elizabeth)*; Fred MacMurray *(Sid)*; Arlene Dahl *(Carol)*; Cornel Wilde *(Bill)*; Elliott Reid *(Tony)*; Margalo Gillmore *(Evelyn)*; Alan Reed *(Tomasco)*; and George Melford, David Hoffman, Eric Wilton.

Opened at the Roxy Theatre, New York, September 28, 1954. Running time, 94 minutes.

Woman's World (also known as *A Woman's World*) was one of those multiple-star films that 20th Century-Fox seemed to favor in the mid-Fifties *(Three Coins in The Fountain, et al.)* and it was done up handsomely in Technicolor and CinemaScope courtesy Joe MacDonald, and boasted a plotty screenplay by old hands Claude Binyon, Mary Loos, and Richard Sale. Jean Negulesco directed with style and pace.

Bacall found herself up against stiff competition this time around, what with Clifton Webb, June Allyson, Van Heflin, and Fred MacMurray in the cast, and her role, while tending to get lost in the shuffle, was a reasonably telling one. The plot has an automobile executive (Clifton Webb) inviting some

Dahl and Bacall register constrasting viewpoints.

Neglectful husband MacMurray senses Bacall's hurt.

of his top field men to his house with their wives, the purpose being to decide which is most suited to the general managership of his company.

Webb, crafty, shrewd, cynical, and sophisticated, analyzes each man, not only as to brainpower and organizational expertise, but as to his domestic and sexual life—the personal as well as professional being, in Webb's philosophy, of equal importance to successful business functioning.

Well, let's see, now—there's Cornel Wilde from Kansas City and his wife, June Allyson, a dowdy but likeable gal. Webb finds Wilde attractive and competent but questions his motivation; it seems neither Wilde nor Allyson want the job for him. Then there's highly talented Van Heflin from Texas, who is afflicted with an overly flirtatious and manipulative wife, played gaudily by Arlene Dahl in décolletage down to *here*.

And then there's Fred MacMurray, an overly ambitious, ulcer-prone guy who puts his work above his personal life to the detriment of his relationship with wife Lauren Bacall. During the visit they arrive at a deeper understanding of their relationship with each other.

All these people come under the tartly observant Webb's close scrutiny, and while he tends to favor Heflin, he becomes concerned that his wife, Dahl (who has tried to barter her sexual favors to Webb

Webb offers a toast. From left to right: Bacall, Elliot Reid, Cornel Wilde, June Allyson, Margalo Gilmore and Van Heflin.

(Right) Wilde and Bacall seem to be checking out their respective mates while dancing.

Bacall and MacMurray.

to further her husband's advancement), will handicap her promising husband's advancement. But when Heflin, aroused fully at last to Dahl's negations, shows firmness in his handling of her, Webb decides that he's the right man for the job.

Wilde and Allyson heave sighs of relief when the decision is made, and prepare to return happily to Kansas, and MacMurray and Bacall realize that the loss of the job means a gain in their chances for a new marital beginning with personal priorities put first.

Bacall is caustic when required, tender and wistful when the plot permits, and multi-dimensional in her moods—in short, one of her better performances. She gets across well the frustration of a devoted but ever-more-impatient wife who feels she plays second-fiddle to her husband's career. MacMurray, who was 46 to Bacall's 30 when they did *Woman's World,* reminds audiences yet again that he was every bit as effective in serious, complex characterizations as he was in his better-known forte, comedy. Webb presides imperially over the proceedings, though even in 1954, given his widely-gossiped-about homosexuality, there was an "inside-joke" element to Dahl's attempted seduction of

Webb gets the couples together to check them out: Bacall, MacMurray, Wilde, June Allyson, Van Heflin, Elliot Reid—Arlene Dahl is seated.

An icy car ride with both lost in their own thoughts.

Bacall and Allyson enjoy Margalo Gilmore's hostessing.

Bacall, glum over her marriage, helps Allyson dress more chicly.

him. But being the fine actor he was, he carried it off convincingly (he played fathers and husbands frequently in that period, always with a fey but amusing flair).

Heflin comes across best, as he limns convincingly a hardworking, talented executive who knows when to draw the line when his flighty wife gets to be too much.

The chemistry between Bacall and Fred MacMurray is positive—despite the aforementioned sixteen-year-difference in their ages, they are a convincing married couple. (Bacall, of course, was in the tenth year of her marriage to the then-55-year-old Bogart, and had given him two kids by 1954. Her handling of her role shows that she knew what she was about here.)

Woman's World was no world-beater or Oscar contender to the 1954 reviewers, but it won its fair share of approval. The women in the audience liked the wardrobes and "woman's angle" complications, and the men enjoyed the business maneuverings, which, though somewhat theatricalized, rang true essentially. Among the critical adjectives: "insightful," "amusingly witty," "sophisticated," "glossy," and "slick."

THE COBWEB

METRO-GOLDWYN-MAYER   1955

Married doctor Widmark has affair with occupational therapist Bacall.

John Kerr, a troubled patient, overhears things.

CREDITS

Vincente Minnelli *(Director)*; John Houseman *(Producer)*; John Paxton *(Screenplay)*; Based on a novel by William Gibson; Leonard Rosenman *(Music)*; Metrocolor; George Folsey *(Photographer)*; Added dialogue by Mr. Gibson; Harold Kress, Editor.

CAST

Richard Widmark *(Dr. Stewart McIver)*; Lauren Bacall *(Meg Rinehart)*; Charles Boyer *(Dr. Douglas N. Devanal)*; Gloria Grahame *(Karen McIver)*; Lillian Gish *(Victoria Inch)*; John Kerr *(Steven Holte)*; Susan Strasberg *(Sue Brett)*; Oscar Levant *(Mr. Capp)*; Tommy Rettig *(Mark)*; Paul Stewart *(Dr. Otto Wolff)*; Jarma Lewis *(Lois Demuth)*; Adele Jergens *(Miss Cobb)*; Bert Freed *(Abe Irwin)*; Edgar Stehli *(Mr. Holcomb)*; Mabel Albertson *(Regina Mitchell-Smythe)*.

Opened at Lowe's State Theatre, New York, August 5, 1955. Running time, 124 minutes.

Bacall went to Metro-Goldwyn-Mayer for the first time in 1955, when she starred with Richard Widmark, Charles Boyer, Lillian Gish, and Gloria Grahame in a sort of *Grand Hotel in the Loony Bin.* Based on a William Gibson novel, produced by John Houseman and directed by Vincente Minnelli (an odd choice for such an assignment), the picture in question, *The Cobweb,* dealt with a series of highly melodramatic (and more than a little confusing) events in a high-class mental clinic, veddy exclusive and high-toned and all that, but also just as depressing and sordid as the lowest reaches of Bellevue.

It's occupational therapy time for staffers Bacall and Widmark.

Gish, the hospital administrator, pours a sherry for Bacall.

Bacall found herself swamped amidst the prestigious casting, and in the not-too-astutely-orchestrated congress of characterizations, hers is one of the weaker ones, not only because the obviously busy Minnelli couldn't give her that much attention, but because her role, as written by John Paxton, is relatively ill-defined and motivationally murky. Suffice it to say that she is an occupational therapist of the more modern school who finds herself having an affair with a married doctor, Richard Widmark, who seeks to introduce more exciting therapeutic techniques to the clinic.

Widmark's ideas run up against the more conservative views of his colleagues (*that* has a familiar ring from many a film before or since), and our hero's problems are furthermore complicated by his marriage to a sluttish creature, Gloria Grahame, whose psychological processes are as loose as her morals.

Charles Boyer is the administrative head of the hospital with liquor and woman problems (it's a long way from *Private Worlds* of twenty years before), and can't do much with a role that is as murkily conceived as Bacall's. John Kerr is a rather sweetly-deranged young man who wanders in and out of the doings of the patient contingent, and Susan Strasberg is another young loony who is sweet and sad as all-get-out. This was Kerr's first picture, and it was an unfortunate debut for him, as his character makes as little sense as, say, that of Oscar Levant, whose least appealing traits as a private individual are made the butt of cruel sport here, as he gulps tranquilizers, displays a prize mother complex, and otherwise disports himself in an undignified (and non-comical) manner.

Lillian Gish comes off best of the lot as the hospital's business manager who is the hapless administrator Boyer's *bete noire*. (Boyer resigns before Gish has the opportunity to really bring him up short.) Gish is forceful, authoritative, no nonsense cynical, and among her advantages in giving a sterling performance is the otherwise-absent-minded screenwriter's gift to her of a well-written, if not especially long, role. More than one critic has commented that Gish emerges the film's real star.

Gish has told, in her autobiography, of an amusing incident while in Hollywood making *The Cobweb,* her first for MGM in decades. While visiting with Ina Claire at director Minnelli's house, Minnelli warned her and Miss Claire that his 8-year-old daughter Liza would give an imitation of both of them—star-struck tot that she was, even then—as soon as they left the house. And that she proceeded to do.

Loony Levant gets sympathy and help from Bacall.

The lovers weather the storm.

All the Metrocolor, all the careful MGM production mounting, all Houseman's producing meticulousness, all Minnelli's frantic ministrations and all of Gish's fine acting couldn't save this film from critical roasting when it was released, "It's so bad it's good" being typical of the reviews. Actually, it holds up better today than at the time it first appeared, but it is still not worth waiting up to see on the late show.

As in *Written on the Wind,* Bacall makes a rather shallow and pallid love interest for Widmark, and in fairness to her, as written, the role would have defied the efforts of the most dynamic star. Nothing much happens to her amidst all the frenetic doings around her, and many Bacall admirers fail to understand why she took the role in the first place.

Widmark has what might be termed the central star role, but while he is charming, charismatic and authoritative, the screenwriter has not made his character a particularly credible or winning one. Gloria Grahame as the minx of the piece is Gish's only possible rival for histrionic plaudits, delivering her usual saucy, perverse, naughty incarnation. But she and her character seem to belong to another picture altogether.

The Cobweb was not a particularly auspicious MGM debut for Bacall. As the studio had already seen better days, with Louis B. Mayer gone four years in 1955, along with the greatest of his stars, it probably didn't matter all that much.

A *New York Times* reviewer, doubtless sympathetic to the evident fact that Bacall had been handed a role that was blurred and weakly written, wrote: "Miss Bacall shrewdly underplays."

BLOOD ALLEY

WARNERS–BATJAC   1955

Bacall in one of the few meditative moments the action-packed script allows her.

Wayne and Bacall are starting to warm up.

Messed-up but on top of it, Bacall's a survivor.

CREDITS

William A. Wellman *(Director)*; A Batjac Production; A.S. Fleischman *(Screenplay)*; Based on his novel; William H. Clothier *(Photographer)*; Alfred Ybarra *(Art Director)*; Roy Webb *(Music)*; Fred MacDowell *(Editor)*. CinemaScope and WarnerColor.

CAST

John Wayne *(Wilder)*; Lauren Bacall *(Cathy Grainger)*; Paul Fix *(Mr. Tso)*; Berry Kroeger *(Old Feng)*; Mike Mazurki *(Big Han)*; Joy Kim *(Susu, Cathy's Maid)*; Anita Ekberg *(Wei Ling)*; W.T. Chang *(Mr. Han)*; George Chan *(Mr. Sing)*; Victor Sen Yung *(Corporal Wang)*.

Opened at neighborhood theatres, New York, October 7, 1955. Running time, 115 minutes.

Lauren Bacall has described John Wayne when he appeared in *Blood Alley,* her first of two films with him, as "to my surprise warm, likable and helpful" and called William Wellman's direction of the movie "salty and terrific." This was the first of the Wayne Batjac productions, which replaced Wayne–Fellows, his earlier company. Robert Mitchum was to have starred originally, but fell out with Wellman after playing one practical joke too many on the crew. After considering Gregory Peck and Bacall's husband, Humphrey Bogart, Wayne decided to star in the film himself, and even helped Wellman with some of the direction while Wellman was temporarily ill.

Blood Alley is typical John Wayne-Versus-the-Communists material, with Wayne, freed from a Communist prison in China by villagers, taking the whole gang with him on a 300-mile boat trip to Hong Kong—a freedom trek, Wayne-style. Along for the ride is Lauren Bacall, in one of her more winning and appealing roles, as a doctor's daughter who almost gets raped by a villainous Oriental. Later she learns that her father has been stoned to death by the Communists. There is some flirtatious hanky-panky between Wayne and Bacall but nothing heavy-going. However, the chemistry between the two is excellent, and they obviously enjoyed acting together.

The story, based on the screenplay (and novel) by A.S. Fleischman, is directed with drive and urgency by Wellman, and the trip down the Formosa Straits—the "Blood Alley" of the title—has more than its share of thrills and suspense. While the band is in the process of escaping in the American-made riverboat, reports of their escape reach the outside world, but the Communist propagandists try to discount and disclaim it. Wayne gets attacked by a pro-Communist family he has taken along out of humanistic concern, and there is a food-poisoning crisis, among many others, but Wayne and Co. make it to their Hong Kong destination.

Blood Alley was yet another of the gung-ho, macho, anti-Communist action films Wayne did frequently, and which made him, a political conservative, the frequent target of liberal groups.

Bacall is serious-minded yet winsomely attractive as the doctor's daughter. Her terror when Wayne saves her from near-rape at the hands of a Chinese officer is limned convincingly. She is also effective in the scene where she learns from Wayne of her father's murder after a rigged Communist trial.

The scene where Wayne slaps Bacall and gets her angry and feisty, just prior to springing the sad news on her, has a contrapuntal vitality and poignancy. Bacall has never looked better (she was 30 when she made *Blood Alley*) and is photographed becomingly by William H. Clothier. Roy Webb's music helps the lively atmospherics along, and the CinemaScope and WarnerColor are assets to the Oriental ambience.

Still, reviewers felt the goings-on had a superficial, comic-book flavor. "Enjoyably escapist but

Bacall worries as the going gets rougher.

Wayne has to tell Bacall her father has been killed; how will he handle it?

nothing beyond that," was typical of the critical comments. "Strictly—indeed solely—for the not too critical and analytical" was another observation. The "Formosa straits" journey was actually filmed at China Camp at San Rafael, and Wellman and Clothier strove for just the right look; the *mise en scène* was, accordingly, surprisingly authentic-looking. The actors among the 189 who get "rescued" by Wayne all looked their parts, and their acting was convincing.

Bacall seems to look back on this picture with favor, chiefly because she enjoyed working with Wayne and Wellman, but it is 80 percent Wayne and 20 percent Bacall, and while her role as written and performed is appealing, it doesn't give Bacall the opportunity to cut loose and ignite as she demon-strates she can do so well in her more suitable roles.

One reviewer commented, "While *Blood Alley* cannot by any means be described as second-rate Wayne, it does not rank among his best pictures either. Possibly because the role was tailored orig-inally to Robert Mitchum's measure, and Wayne had to jump in practically at the last minute, he seems to go through his paces with a more perfunctory manner and less robust enthusiasm than is his usual wont. He has done more exciting fare than this, but *Blood Alley* has its share of thrills." The reviewer added, "Lauren Bacall, likeable as she is in her role, is along for the ride this time more as leading lady than as co-star, but her appearance here won't set back her career."

The Villagers, Bacall, and Wayne get acquainted.

WRITTEN ON THE WIND

UNIVERSAL   1956

CREDITS

Douglas Sirk *(Director)*; Albert Zugsmith *(Producer)*; George Zuckerman *(Screenplay)*; Based on a novel by Robert Wilder; Color by Technicolor.

CAST

Rock Hudson *(Mitch Wayne)*; Lauren Bacall *(Lucy Moore Hadley)*; Robert Stack *(Kyle Hadley)*; Dorothy Malone *(Marylee Hadley)*; Robert Keith *(Jasper Hadley)*; Grant Williams *(Bill Miley)*; Robert J. Wilke *(Dan Willis)*; Edward C. Platt *(Dr. Paul Cochrane)*; Harry Shannon *(Hoak Wayne)*; John Larch *(Ray Carter)*; Joseph Granby *(R. J. Courtney)*.

Opened at the Capitol Theatre, New York, January 11, 1957. (Released in Los Angeles in December, 1956.) Running time, 99 minutes.

As in *Cobweb* the year before, Bacall found herself in a rather thankless romantic lead that made little or no use of her inherent wit and pungency, this time playing off Rock Hudson. The meaty roles went to Robert Stack and Dorothy Malone, whose vivid, gaudy performance won her the 1956 supporting actress Academy Award.

Written on the Wind, is a bitingly melodramatic cake of sour soap that over the past thirty years has had an equal share of admirers and detractors. Stack gives perhaps the best performance of his lacklustre career as a Texas oil heir who elopes (in his private plane, of course) with New York secretary Bacall. Along for the ride is Stack's pal from boyhood, Rock Hudson, and the attraction between the new bride and geologist Hudson blossoms from the start—albeit platonically.

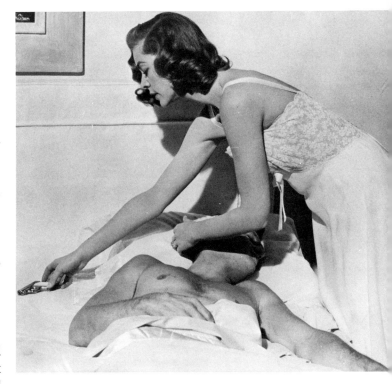

She removes gun from tormented Stack's bed.

Bacall finds her love for Hudson is growing.

Witchy Malone cracks wise while Bacall waxes tense.

Bacall and Hudson gradually get acquainted.

Back in Texas, Stack soon becomes paranoid, doubting his manhood, especially when a doctor calls his sperm-count "weak," thus ruling-out potential fatherhood. He does get Bacall pregnant, but imagines the baby is Hudson's, and hell breaks loose at the Texas mansion, with tormented Stack physically abusing hapless Bacall, and sterling Hudson becoming her protector and, gradually, light o' love.

Then there is Stack's nymphomaniac sister, Dorothy Malone, a spoiled playgirl who gets into constant scrapes with the men, and who has nurtured an obsessive abiding love for Hudson since childhood. Hudson sees them only as brother and sister, however. Robert Keith is the family patriarch who dies of a heart attack while Malone plays loud fast music after one of her misadventures.

Stack, of course, conveniently dies, leaving Bacall and Hudson to flee the mansion, whose only remaining inhabitant is a suddenly sobered Malone, in a finely-tailored, mannishly-styled suit, sitting at her daddy's old desk and fingering (to considerable audience hilarity) a phallic-shaped oil-derrick model.

Director Douglas Sirk has managed to make some of the melodramatic excesses compelling and highly watchable in a good-bad movie way, and Malone's vivid, Bette Davis-ish bad-girl-with-perverse-instincts-but-longing-romantic-heart is certainly that highly talented, but not always wisely handled actress's cinematic high point.

Though naughty as hell and mean as sin throughout most of the movie, Malone registers authentic poignancy in one scene when she visits a childhood spot where she recalls her original love for Hudson.

Stack, wild-eyed, distraught and humiliated throughout the film, not only by his imagined lack of potency but his constant self-deprecation in contrast to Hudson, whom he considers more virile and "with-it," is a compelling figure indeed. He proved a surprise to 1956 audiences, who up to then had associated him with charming, bland, also-ran filmic contributions. Many felt Stack deserved a supporting Oscar every bit as much as Malone, but Oscar-time vagaries ruled otherwise.

Robert Keith, who was always an incisive, well-disciplined character actor (most notably with Susan Hayward in *My Foolish Heart*), gets across all the bewilderment of a hardworking, ambitious tycoon who finds himself sadly disappointed in his children, Stack and Malone.

Bacall is unfortunately cast in the role of a passive *reactor* to the more colorful characters (as written) around her. George Zuckerman's script doesn't give her much leeway emotionally or allow her any pointedness of characterization. In a sense, this is a

A lighter moment for two who are destined for love.

A pregnant Bacall lies stricken while Hudson phones for help.

141

The triangular leads, high in the sky.

Insecure Stack needles his wife and Hudson.

waste, because it is interesting to speculate how well *she* might have performed Malone's role—especially in view of her perverse and tart rendition of another variety of "bad girl" in *Young Man With a Horn* six years earlier.

Hudson is charming and manly, but he, too, must play a relatively pallid and tame second fiddle to the emotional pyrotechnics and confrontational *tour-de-forces* that Malone and Stack pull off effectively with screenwriter Zuckerman's help. Zuckerman adapted the story from a novel by Robert Wilder.

The color effects are notably handsome, but one wonders whether the garish but essentially somber theme might not have profited more from black-and-white lensing.

Written on the Wind was produced during the gathering storm of Humphrey Bogart's final year of crucial illness, as was the film that followed it, *Designing Woman.* Which leads to the question of whether Bacall could have done full justice to a more demanding and complex role, given the deepening crisis in her private life.

DESIGNING WOMAN

METRO-GOLDWYN-MAYER   1957

CREDITS

Vincente Minnelli *(Director)*; Dore Schary *(Producer)*; George Wells *(Associate Producer)*; George Wells *(Screenplay)*; Based on a Suggestion by Helen Rose; Andre Previn *(Music)*; John Alton *(Photographer)*; Helen Rose *(Gowns)*; Adrienne Fazan *(Editor)*. CinemaScope. Metrocolor.

CAST

Gregory Peck *(Mike Hagen)*; Lauren Bacall *(Marilla Hagen)*; Dolores Gray *(Lori Shannon)*; Sam Levene *(Ned Hammerstein)*; Tom Helmore *(Zachary Wilde)*; Mickey Shaughnessy *(Maxie Stulz)*; Jesse White *(Charlie Arneg)*; Chuck Connors *(Johnnie "O")*; Edward Platt *(Martin J. Daylor)*; Alvy Moore *(Luke Coslow)*; Carol Veazie *(Gwen)*; Jack Cole *(Randy Owen)*.

Opened at Radio City Music Hall, May 16, 1957. Running time, 118 minutes.

Bacall has described *Designing Woman* as "a lovely, funny script, a terrific part," and recalls that she was happy to be working again and felt lucky to get the role, which Grace Kelly had refused because she was about to marry Prince Rainier. Bacall shot the film in the months just before Bogart died, and remembers that she was reluctant to leave him, but he insisted she take the role, and eagerly listened to her reports on it when she came home at night.

Designer Helen Rose, who had suggested the idea to the studio (it was to be Dore Schary's final MGM film), designed no less than 132 gowns for Bacall in this, and the critics declared that she

Bacall broods about unpredictable, wandering husband Peck.

Peck and Bacall in a more relaxed, romantic moment.

Peck obviously doesn't approve of what is being served up.

looked sleek and spiffy in all of them. Her light, gay, seemingly effortless performance and fine comic timing under Vincente Minnelli's expert direction are all the more remarkable considering the heavy stresses on her at home during Bogart's final illness.

The plot was one of those affairs that Spencer Tracy and Katharine Hepburn in an earlier MGM period would have found perfectly tailored to their measure. It involves a sports writer on a newspaper (Gregory Peck) and a highstyle fashion designer (Bacall) who get together despite *her* importunate Broadway producer suitor, and *his* hot and heavy involvement with a musical comedy star. Tom Helmore and Dolores Gray do ample justice to these roles, respectively. Bacall and Peck marry, he runs into difficulty in permanently disentangling himself from Miss Gray (who in a restaurant scene that by now has become a cliché, dumps a plate of ravioli in his lap when she gets her dander up), plus other complications that have them first together, then apart, then finally reunited.

During the course of the 118-minute screen time, Bacall must fend off advances from the producer, and Peck runs afoul of mobsters. Mickey Shaughnessy is on hand as an ex-pug assigned as bodyguard to Peck, and dancer Jack Cole stops the show by dancing all over the mobsters' faces, Apache-style, in a back-alley fight to beat all fights.

Of course Helen Rose managed to get in a mammoth fashion show in the most elaborate Metro-Goldwyn-Mayer manner (even as late as 1957 they hadn't forgotten how to serve it up).

The plot was reminiscent of many a movie that had gone before it, but director Minnelli kept things soufflé-light, and Bacall turned in a dandy performance, though the critics were divided on her, Peck, and some aspects of the film.

Settling down to more serious business.

Gregory Peck was yet again grossly miscast. The year before, he had attempted Melville's *Moby Dick*, and demonstrated a woeful lack of passion and fire and demonic vitality that the role of Captain Ahab cried out for, and that John Barrymore had gotten across so tellingly in previous versions. Later he was to essay the role of F. Scott Fitzgerald in *Beloved Enemy*, and again he proved to be no one's idea of the complex, mercurial author of *The Great Gatsby*.

Now here and again was Peck trying to make like Spencer Tracy in a Tracy role, and he demonstrated that he lacked Tracy's comedy timing, ease, throwaway style, and mandatory lightness of touch. A handsome, masculine, sexy-looking actor with a winning, muted, unassertive style, Peck was often rushed into roles for which he was unsuited to cash in on his star chemistry and sex appeal. His Mike Hagen was, unfortunately, yet another of those roles.

I personally admired Bacall in *Designing Woman*, and felt she did as well as Hepburn could have; she is tart, alluring, handsomely dressed and coiffured,

The dog steals this scene, but Bacall's mind is elsewhere anyway.

Tom Helmore and Jack Cole seem to find Bacall one handful of woman here.

Looks like permanent packing, but she ends up on home base.

and demonstrates a command of comic nuance. Some critics of the time did not agree with me. Bosley Crowther in *The New York Times* wrote: "There is something a little chilly and forbidding about Miss Bacall." William K. Zinsser in *The New York Herald-Tribune,* on the other hand, was generous to Peck and fair to Bacall when he declared, "[They] make a handsome and attractive pair and they extract whatever humor lurks in the story," adding, "Miss Bacall looks very satisfying in all those gowns designed by Helen Rose."

It is interesting to speculate how Bacall would have matched up in this film with Spencer Tracy in his prime; Tracy probably would have brought out added facets to her performance via sheer chemistry-osmosis. As it was, Peck, who, to be fair, could be very fine in roles tailored to his measure *(Keys of the Kingdom, Valley of Decision, Spellbound, et al.)* could not but dampen the Bacall verve slightly here.

Stack and Bacall were awash in goo, as a couple facing Death's Parting.

THE GIFT OF LOVE

20TH CENTURY-FOX   1958

CREDITS

Jean Negulesco *(Director)*; Charles Brackett *(Producer)*; Luther Davis *(Screenplay)*; From a story by Nelia Gardner White; Milton Krasner *(Photographer)*; Cyril Mockridge *(Music)*; Song by Sammy Fain and Paul Francis Webster; a remake of *Sentimental Journey* (1946, 20th-Fox), also from a story by Ms. White; CinemaScope–DeLuxe Color.

CAST

Lauren Bacall *(Julie Beck)*; Robert Stack *(Bill Beck)*; Evelyn Rudie *(Hitty)*; Lorne Greene *(Grant Allan)*; Anne Seymour *(McMasters)*; Edward Platt *(Dr. Miller)*; Joseph Kearns *(Mr. Rynicker)*.

Opened at the Paramount Theatre, New York, February 11, 1958. Running time, 105 minutes.

Nobody—but nobody—particularly liked *The Gift of Love,* including its star, who dismissed it in retrospect as "not a marvelous picture—a remake, sentimental." It was Bacall's first picture since Bogart's death, and someone at 20th Century-Fox—an ill-advised soul indeed—got the brainstorm that a remake of the 1946 John Payne-Maureen O'Hara weeper, *Sentimental Journey,* would be just right for Bacall, whose widowhood was fresh in the minds of the American public. The sly and tasteless commercial thinking that underlay the renascence of the tale for Mrs. Humphrey Bogart reflects little credit on the studio movers-and-shakers—and many wondered why Bacall herself went along with it.

The explanation is probably that Bacall needed to get back to work to forget, and *The Gift of Love* was

the best of a weak field of films offered to her at the time. The same geniuses who dreamed up this gimmick also decided that Robert Stack, who had ignited so eloquently as Bacall's deranged, tormented husband in *Written on the Wind,* would be perfect for a return engagement opposite her. Both ideas turned out to be less than brilliant.

Sentimental Journey had been calculated to wring the tears out of the post-war 1946 audience, so conditioned to death and loss after the horrors and sorrows of the 1941-45 World War, but even in 1946 the tale came on as hopelessly, archly maudlin. Even women members of the audience reportedly registered impatience with it during screenings, but "soap—any kind of soap—sells" was the watchword in 1946. "Soap Sells" was revived in 1958—a somewhat more cynical year, granted—when the 20th-Fox boys were confronted with the Bacall widowhood, which they hoped, as before noted, to exploit for audience weepiness. Cynicism, thy name is Hollywood—but the women viewers of 1958 refused to be taken in, and *The Gift of Love* was a resounding flop.

She's going to die—and what will *become* of him.

Bacall waves sweetly to Stack

Stack, kid actress Evelyn Rudie, and Bacall walking nowhere in particular.

Is Stack getting fed up with things? With Philip Ober.

And what was the plot? A childless couple adopt a strange little girl (they were a producer and actress in the 1946 original, a physicist and his wife in the 1958 replay). It seems wifie is dying and she wants to leave hubby something cute and little to love him when she is no longer around. She then dies of a heart condition and man and child find they are incompatible—he being a practical scientist type and she an imaginative fantasist by nature. Well, it seems (we're writing about the 1958 picture now) that she was gotten from an orphanage, and the widower, having had his fill, sends her back there. Later he has second thoughts, and they get back together as dad and daughter, and Stack realizes that the child (played by Evelyn Rudie) is truly Bacall's posthumous "gift of love."

The 1946 film had been directed by Walter Lang, from a saccharine story by Nelia Gardner White. In 1958 the director was Jean Negulesco, with whom Bacall enjoyed working, and 20th Century-Fox producer Charles Brackett proceeded to assault his audiences for 105 endless minutes with CinemaScope and DeLuxe Color by Milton Krasner, music by Cyril Mockridge, a song by Sammy Fain and Paul Francis Webster dragged in to save the day (but which failed to do so,) a tear-drenched, blatantly unsubtle screenplay by Luther Davis (again from the Nelia Gardner White original,) and a hairdo and array of clothes that seemed to handicap Bacall rather than highlight her.

The studio reasoning behind all this was probably (in addition to the aforementioned wrongheaded thinking) that Bacall the Widow should be presented, in her cinematic advent in the Post-Bogart period, as a charming, sensitive, mystically-oriented wife and mother, so that the 1958 lady viewers could cry into their Kleenex over the real-life pain and loss of it all, but what was overlooked

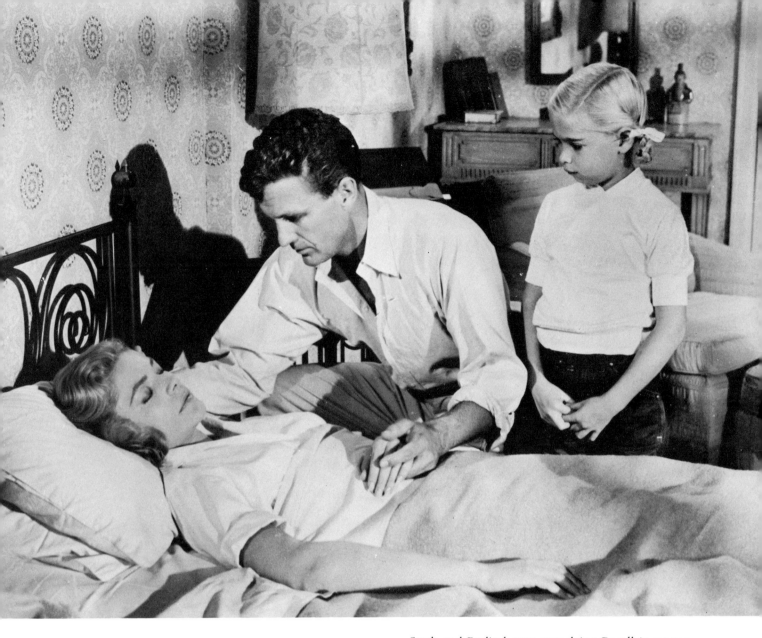

Stack and Rudie hover over dying Bacall in weepy scene.

was that Bacall registered most vividly on-screen in roles that were racy, a little bitchy, a little naughty, and more than a little pungent.

Accordingly this tear-drenched mishmash proved an unfortunate vehicle for the Bacall of 1958. The plot contrivances and syrupy dialogue drowned out the tart saltiness of the Bacall incarnation of, say, *How to Marry a Millionaire,* and had a knowing, sharp "spiritualist" been able to set up a line between the departed Bogie and "Baby" as of that year, he probably would have whispered across the void, "Baby, don't do it!" But she did do it, and *it* did nothing for her. "Weepy," "silly," "maudlin," "inexplicable miscasting," "soap at its worst," "arch," "coy"—all these were critical reactions to *TGOL.* As for Robert Stack, he found no chances to ignite in his distinctive style, drowned as he was in all the goo. *The Gift of Love* is seldom revived—and that is a saving grace.

FLAME OVER INDIA

20TH CENTURY-FOX–J. ARTHUR RANK   1960

CREDITS

CREDITS

J. Lee Thompson *(Director)*; Marcel Hellman *(Producer)*; Geoffrey Unsworth *(Photographer)*; CinemaScope–DeLuxe Color; A J. Arthur Rank release (originally titled *Northwest Frontier*); Robin Estridge *(Screenplay)*.

CAST

Lauren Bacall *(Catherine Wyatt)*; Kenneth More *(Captain Scott)*; Herbert Lom *(Van Leyden)*; Wilfrid Hyde-White *(Mr. Bridie)*; Gorind Raja Ross *(Prince Kishan)*; Ian Hunter *(John Windham)*; John Gwillim *(Brigadier Ames)*; Ursula Jeans *(Lady Windham)*; I.S. Johar *(Gupta)*; Eugene Decker *(Mr. Peters)*.

Opened at the Paramount Theatre, New York, April 29, 1960. Running time, 130 minutes.

Flame Over India was one of Bacall's more felicitous assignments. She recalls that she thoroughly enjoyed doing the picture. It was shot, she remembers, first for a week in London, then to India for six weeks, Spain for the next six, wrapping up in London again. She loved India. "I was in a place far from anything I'd known, my attitude was open, abandoned; it was high adventure and I loved it."

She was also in fine acting fettle while doing the film, and the critics were, for the most part, kind to her. Howard Thompson in *The New York Times* wrote: "The acting is consistently good and restrained....Miss Bacall is personable and workmanlike." Paul V. Beckley in *The New York Herald-Tribune* observed that "the stress is as much on character as on action, and if there is a romance

She is protective toward the young prince (Gordino Raja Ross), determined to get him to safety.

With her charge in a quieter moment before danger strikes.

between Miss Bacall and Kenneth More, it does not sap any of the essential energy of the chase but grows quite naturally and credibly out of the circumstances in which they find themselves."

Beckley also referred favorably to the "sharp script and controlled direction by J. Lee Thompson," and called *Flame Over India* (original title: *Northwest Frontier;* Rank changed it for fear it would be regarded as an American Western) "one of the best things of its kind to come along in some time."

Flame Over India features my second-favorite Bacall performance (after *Young Man With a Horn).* As an intrepid American governess helping her charge, a young Indian Prince, to escape Moslem rebels via a wild train chase across India, with intrepid British officer Kenneth More along to aid her, she is forthright, dynamic, enterprising, and wonderfully self-possessed and confident. As she plays her, governess Catherine Wyatt is made of sturdy stuff; she is adaptable and, when the situation calls for it, courageous. Nor is her womanly nature impervious to the masculine charisma of brave officer More, with a romance (of sorts) developing out of the shared experience, with all of its harrowing sidelights.

There is much of a Kiplingesque flavor to the proceedings; it opens in high gear with the Moslem rebels storming a British stronghold and attempting to invade the young Indian prince's palace with intent to murder him. Bacall and More spirit the boy onto an old railroad train; the engine that pulls it, called The Empress of India, is a marvelous Victorian contraption (the time is turn of the century) that commands almost as much attention as the star performers.

Across India they go, along with other refugees, hostile forces all around them. The characters on board include a sinister munitions salesman, a high-

Time is of the essence, with danger ever nearer.

Exiting the palace a step ahead of the murderous rebels.

powered Dutch journalist, an English noblewoman, etc. There are continuous skirmishes with pursuing horsemen; the rebels blow up the track but enterprising More and aides quickly and ingeniously repair it; they make it over a dangerous gorge; a traitor on board makes one final attempt on the child-prince's life. The action is vivid and continuous and inventive, and when the tired but elated group finally make it to safety and friendly hands, the viewer feels he has personally participated in their compellingly limned travail.

J. Lee Thompson has given audiences not just a thrilling action picture, set in actual-Indian ambiences and photographed in tasteful color and CinemaScope, but a story of great distinction with all the characters convincing and dimensional. Among the fine actors on hand are Wilfrid Hyde-White, the distinguished British character actor, in another of his fey, charming roles; Ian Hunter; Ursula Jeans; Herbert Lom (the villain of the piece, of course); young Gorind Raja Ross as the terrified but game prince who forms a strong bond with

Her heart goes out to a helpless baby admidst the carnage.

Ian Hunter meets the prince as More and Bacall
exchange worried looks.

Bacall and More during the trip; John Gwillim as a
brigadier; and I.S. Johar, the Indian actor, who plays
the engineer.

The *Tribune*'s Beckley felt that *Flame Over India*
contained something for folks of all ages, adding,
"although [adult] audiences should find this stirring
enough, young audiences should find it fascinating," and Howard Thompson of the *Times* added,
somewhat in dissent, "[it] is an absorbing and
picturesque, if unsurprising, film journey."

The chemistry between Bacall and More is affecting and convincing; though their growing feeling for
each other is conveyed subtly and couched in
shared-effort-toward-the-goal-of-safety terms, it is all
the more touching and winning because of this
understatement. *Flame Over India,* like all well-
made action films with strong human characterizations, leaves one with a good feeling.

Bacall is a Psychiatrist with a purpose.

SHOCK TREATMENT

20TH CENTURY-FOX–ARCOLA 1964

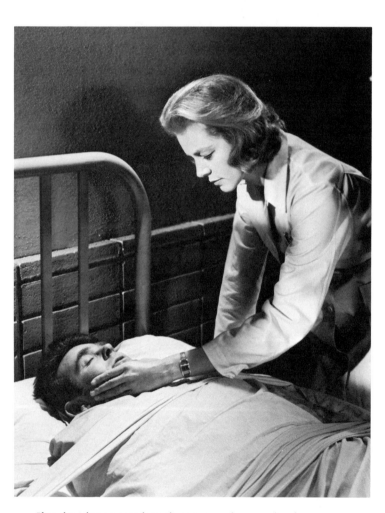

She decides to test her dangerous drug on hapless Whitman.

CREDITS

Denis Sanders *(Director)*; Aaron Rosenberg *(Producer)*; Sydney Boehm *(Screenplay)*; From the book by Winfred Van Atta; Sam Leavitt *(Photographer)*; Jack Martin Smith *(Art Director)*; Jerry Goldsmith *(Music)*; Louis R. Loeffler *(Editor)*. CinemaScope.

CAST

Stuart Whitman *(Dale Nelson)*; Carol Lynley *(Cynthia)*; Roddy McDowall *(Martin Ashley)*; Lauren Bacall *(Dr. Edwina Beigley)*; Olive Deering *(Mrs. Mellon)*; Ossie Davis *(Capshaw)*; Donald Buka *(Psychologist)*; Pauline Myers *(Dr. Walden)*; Evadne Baker *(Intern)*; Robert J. Wilke *(Newton)*; Bert Freed *(Josephson)*; Judson Laire *(Harley Manning)*; Judith De Hart *(Matron)*; Lili Clark *(Alice)*; Douglas Dumbrille *(Judge)*.

Opened at Loew's Neighborhood Theatres, New York, July 22, 1964. Running time, 94 minutes.

Bacall returned to the screen after four years in a film many thought unworthy of her. What might have made a biting and dynamic film about chicaneries in a mental hospital, with Bacall as a psychiatrist out to grind her own particular axe, fell short of genuine craftsmanship, and what excitement there was tended toward the shoddy and slapdash.

Howard Thompson of *The New York Times* wrote: "Minus its spooky music, the general tone of bland sensationalism, and a pat, almost farcical, ending, this slick picture might have made a genuinely suspenseful chiller."

Kathleen Carroll of the New York *Daily News* opined: "Lauren Bacall is her ever-cool self as a psychiatrist obsessed with the desire for money to facilitate her rather unorthodox research projects."

Billed fourth below Stuart Whitman, Carol Lynley, and Roddy McDowall, Bacall testifies at McDowall's trial for murder and gets him committed to a mental hospital for observation. McDowall has done away with his wealthy employer, and the executor suspects he is pretending insanity and has hidden a million dollars that the dead woman kept in cash.

Stuart Whitman plays an actor hired by executor Judson Laire to fake mental illness, facilitate his own commitment, and then determine where McDowall hid the money. Bacall suspects something fishy about Whitman. McDowall, under hypnosis, has confessed to Bacall that he has a lot of money, and Bacall, who wants the money for her recondite research projects, tries to locate it. It seems that she has up her sleeve a super-powerful drug that produces permanent catatonia in animals and she is just dying to try it on a human being, so she railroads Whitman into guinea-pig experiments. He develops catatonic spells.

He escapes, finds that the executor has died, and discovers McDowall and Bacall digging up the money. Bacall, obsessed with getting the cash to promote her experiments, goes wacko when she discovers it has burned to ashes, and winds up committed to the hospital herself. Whitman goes free, and Carol Lynley, a patient who has weathered manic depression, and with whom Whitman has fallen in love, is discharged as cured.

Such is the rather longwinded plot. Whitman, Lynley, McDowall and other good actors try hard to inject some meaningfulness into it all, but the wildly melodramatic elements eventually defeat them. Bacall is sharp, decisive, and intense, then has a field

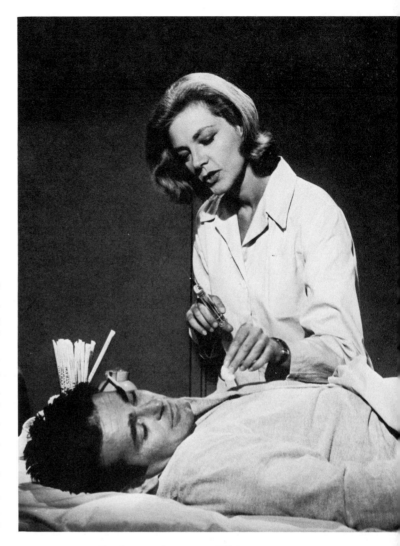
Getting ready to turn Whitman into a catatonic.

McDowall spills the money beans to Bacall.

Determined to get her point across.

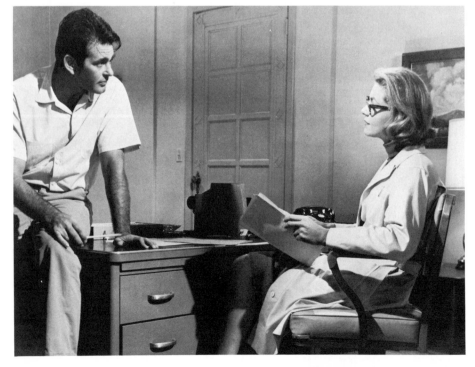

Mutually suspicious Whitman and Bacall size each other up.

day of sorts as her mind crumbles. She has managed to convey with her eyes and gestures and speech patterns throughout the picture that something wild and far-out will eventually happen to her. Of course, it does.

A lot of people wondered why she chose the picture and role after such a long absence from the screen, which perforce demanded that she come back with, and in, something strong and surefire. She has indicated that she was intrigued by the idea of a female psychiatrist so obsessed with her experiments that, when frustrated in the pursuit of them for lack of research funds, she goes literally mad. The possibilities for acting fireworks doubtless would have attracted any serious actress, but she didn't reckon with the thin screenplay, the uninspired direction of Sanders, and other elements that kept the picture from looking Class A.

In her autobiography she admitted: "I lowered my professional sights totally to start working in pictures again, and agreed to be in a truly tacky movie, *Shock Treatment,* whose only saving grace was that my friend Roddy McDowall would be in it and we could suffer together."

In one of her interviews back in the 1960s, she said of *Shock Treatment* that she had felt at the time that Sidney Boehm's screenplay, with all its limitations, had just enough in it that she might be able to exploit for felicitous histrionic results. So she might have felt, after all, that there were, at least originally, other potential "saving graces" to the film besides friend Roddy. The result was a disappointment.

"If they must do mental hospital stuff," one critic wrote, "they will have to learn out Hollywood way to mix the melodrama and the mental stuff so that they blend convincingly. Bacall, McDowall, Whitman and Lynley work hard, but they are defeated by the director and writer. Too bad."

McDowall has the money, and Bacall wants it. So does Whitman.

SEX AND THE SINGLE GIRL

WARNER BROTHERS   1964

Fonda and Bacall mix it up.

CREDITS

Richard Quine *(Director)*; William T. Orr *(Producer)*; Joseph Heller *(Screenplay)*; inspired by Helen Gurley Brown's *Sex and the Single Girl;* from a story by Joseph Hoffman; Charles Lang *(Photographer)*; David Wages *(Editor)*; Technicolor and Panavision. Title song by Quine and Neal Hefti.

CAST

Tony Curtis *(Bob Weston)*; Natalie Wood *(Helen Brown)*; Henry Fonda *(Frank Broderick)*; Lauren Bacall *(Sylvia Broderick)*; Mel Ferrer *(Rudy)*; Fran Jeffries *(Gretchen)*; Leslie Parrish *(Susan)*; Edward Everett Horton *(The Chief)*; Larry Storch *(Motorcycle Cop)*; Howard St. John *(George Randall)*; Otto Kruger *(Dr. Anderson)*; William Lanteau *(Sylvester)*.

Opened at the Rivoli and TransLux 52nd Street theatres, New York. December 26, 1964. Running time, 114 minutes.

As what one reviewer called a "screaming, screeching, chinaware-throwing shrew," Bacall, along with Henry Fonda, who played her husband, stole *Sex and the Single Girl* away from the other actors. Howard Thompson of *The New York Times* led the chorus of critical approval, with these words: "Miss Bacall and Mr. Fonda suavely steal the show...as [Tony Curtis's] scrappy neighbors, they supply the real spice and fun, especially Miss Bacall, who has the wittiest lines and all but pierces the picture with her buzzsaw growl."

Bacall herself never held the film in high esteem, despite her excellent showing in it, dismissing it

Bacall kibitzes as Fonda monkeys around.

Wood and Bacall contemplate mixed indentities.

succinctly with the words, "a very good cast—Natalie Wood, Hank Fonda, Tony Curtis—but not a good film" Among other personal encomiums to Bacall: "The real acting honors go to Fonda and Bacall," "the cast plays it for laughs that aren't always there," and "fairly amusing tale…Bacall and Fonda wrap it up as a battling married couple."

My own reaction to *SASG* was that without Bacall and Fonda it would have been thin, lightweight stuff indeed, a foolish film cynically and crassly attempting to batten off the title of Helen Gurley's then-popular book—and with title song, no less, a song that twenty-two years have shown to have been indeed a fizzle.

Bacall makes things sparkle again and again—but unfortunately isn't given the opportunity to do it as often as needed. She is extremely amusing discussing mistaken identities with Miss Wood (who plays a psychologist who has put out a book on sexual mores, and is being wooed by scandal-mag publisher Curtis, whose publication had panned the book). And she and Fonda sparkle, snap, pop, and effervesce in a nightclub scene in which they cavort with clowning insouciance. And when these two get down to some good old-fashioned domestic brawling, their faces screwed up into angry caricatures of hell-let-loose, they practically jump off the screen into the audience like a couple of forces of nature.

The trouble here is that Bacall and Fonda are hobbled by an inane, foolish, and often dull and confused plot that fails to make even elementary sense, and as directed by Richard Quine (maybe dreaming up that foolish title song depleted his energies), the film defies salvaging operations—that is, if anyone at 20th had entertained them after seeing it in the screening room.

As for Helen Gurley Brown, whose book title was dragged in to titillate the more curious and prurient folk in the fifty states, Canada, and England, she tried in some interviews to be tactful about the film, but to many of her friends expressed her outrage and disgust at the cynicisms and bowdlerizations implicit in the whole dreary project. And Joseph Heller should have gone to the South Seas to hide, considering the messy pastiche of plotting he served up in his screenplay.

We recount the plot herewith, as an example to all screenwriting students in schools nationwide of what *not* to do when writing a film:

Well, it seems that Curtis operates a nasty scandal mag called *Dirt,* and he has published a sensational piece on Wood, a research psychologist who has written a book called—guess what? He wants to interview the lady, but she will have none of it.

Keeping it lively on the dance floor.

Curtis then maneuvers to impersonate a neighbor, Fonda, and goes to Wood for "marriage counselling." A lot of silly, unnecessarily complicated seduction nonsense follows, featuring a mutual tumble into a boat basin, attempts by Curtis to get Wood drunk with multiple martinis, etc.

When Wood finally falls for the guy, and Tony reveals that after all the marriage-and-wifie confessional-couch stuff, he is not married, she thinks he is lying; Wood goes to see Bacall, who thinks she's talking about her real hubby, Fonda, and Curtis sends his secretary and his former girl friend to Wood; she summons Bacall, and the three women all show up at once (are you following this mishmash?). Next thing we know, Bacall is having Fonda arrested for bigamy; Wood (whose name is Helen Brown, of course) ditches Curtis for Mel Ferrer; Curtis gets fired from the mag when he refuses to discredit Wood, with whom he is solidly in love; and after a freeway and airport chase, with Bacall pursuing Fonda and Curtis following Wood, all the right people get sorted out and put together.

A mess, isn't it? But thanks to the Almighty for Miss Bacall and Mr. Fonda.

HARPER

WARNER BROTHERS   1966

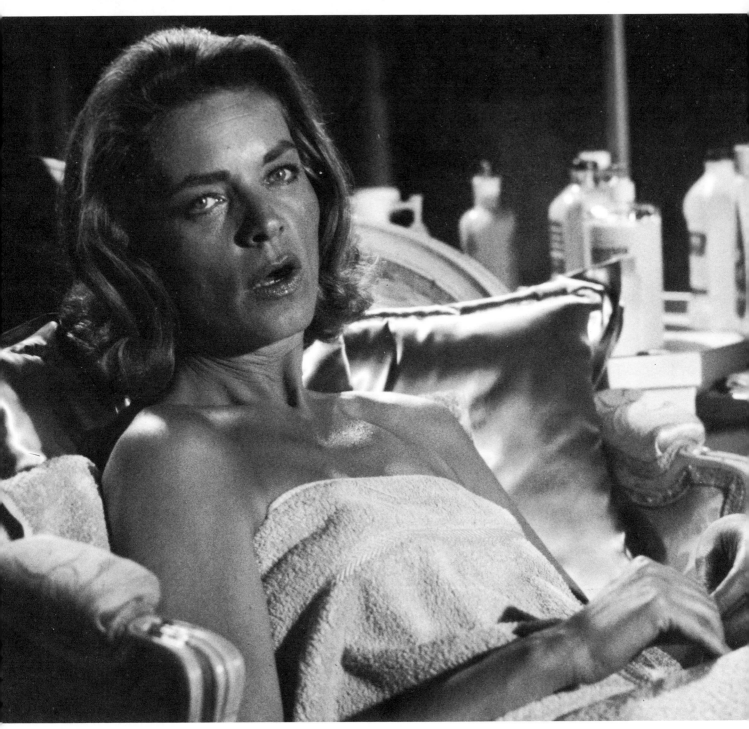

Bacall plays a shrewish wife bitchily.

CREDITS

Jack Smight *(Director)*; A Jerry Gershwin–Elliott Kastner Production; William Goldman *(Screenplay)*; Based on the novel *The Moving Target,* by Ross MacDonald; Johnny Mandel *(Music)*; Conrad Hall *(Photographer)*; Stefan Arnsten *(Editor)*. Technicolor and Panavision.

CAST

Paul Newman *(Lew Harper)*; Lauren Bacall *(Mrs. Sampson)*; Julie Harris *(Betty Fraley)*; Arthur Hill *(Albert Graves)*; Janet Leigh *(Susan Harper)*; Pamela Tiffin *(Miranda Sampson)*; Robert Wagner *(Alan Taggert)*; Robert Webber *(Dwight Troy)*; Shelley Winters *(Fay Estabrook)*; Strother Martin *(Claude)*; Jacqueline DeWit *(Mrs. Kronberg)*; China Lee *(Bunny Dancer)*.

Opened at the Forum, RKO 58th Street and RKO 23rd Street theatres, New York, March 30, 1966. Running time, 121 minutes.

Based on Ross MacDonald's *The Moving Target* (that title was used in England,) *Harper* showcases Paul Newman in the type of private-eye role that the late Humphrey Bogart had made famous. Many critics made the comparison in Bogart's favor, commenting that Newman's technique here was more superficial and show biz than Bogart's, who remained in their view the undisputed master of the genre. Newman, they opined, lacked the Master's "cool" and dispassionate fatalism and detached ruefulness. Bacall was reportedly hired as an "in" joke, since she had not only been Mrs. Bogart but had figured onscreen in a Bogart private-eye drama, *The Big Sleep.*

William Schoell in a retrospective review in *Quirk's Reviews,* wrote of Bacall in this: "[She] is deliciously bitchy, and her verbal swordsplay with Pamela Tiffin is hilarious." Bosley Crowther in *The New York Times* said, "Miss Bacall is her usual sharp-clawed feline in the unclear role of the wife," and Bob Salmaggi wrote of Bacall, who hires private-eye Newman to find her missing alcoholic husband, "the man's couldn't-care-less wife [is] coolly and bitchily played."

Bacall later recalled the picture thus: "I was offered a part in *Harper* with Paul Newman—a kind of suspense film patterned after *The Big Sleep,* but without the same kind of part for me. Paul was the detective. I knew him, liked him personally and as an actor, and was more than pleased to have an opportunity to work with him. That would take up a month in the summer [of 1965]." The film was released the following March (1966).

I personally found the film thin and contrived, and without its fine cast and the major efforts they put into it, it wouldn't have amounted to much. That cast included such heavyweight talents as Julie Harris, Shelley Winters, Janet Leigh, and Arthur Hill, with Pamela Tiffin, Robert Wagner, Robert Webber, and Strother Martin also in there trying hard. This formidable array of talent, plus a shrewd advertising and promotional campaign, and the potent Newman box office chemistry, succeeded in turning a doubtful project into a success. I found Newman competent and attractive, but Bogart he was not, and the doings seem perfunctory and mechanical during much of the footage in which he appears. This is due partly to Smight's workmanlike but hardly inspired direction, and the William Goldman screenplay, which failed to catch completely the spirit of Ross MacDonald's original. And the elaborate Technicolor and Panavision photographic work of Conrad Hall seemed to distract from, rather than promote, the mixed-up doings, which cried out for stark, somber black-and-white—another case of 1966-style production gloss triumphing over atmospheric credibility.

I concede that my opinion of Newman in this evolved over the years; seeing it more recently, I find that my original view of it requires modification, both as to the film and his performance.

Estranged from his wife, Janet Leigh, Newman is assigned by cynical, bitchy Mrs. Sampson to locate her missing husband who, she tartly informs one and all, "is worth twenty million on the hoof." Her attitude, as limned by Bacall, is not only couldn't-care-less but smoulderingly contemptuous.

After receipt of a half-million-dollar ransom demand, Bacall makes it rather obvious that her husband matters nothing to her, and that she'd just as soon see him dead. It turns out that missing hubby, as Newman discovers, is just that—dead as a doornail. Bacall is not on particularly warm terms with her stepdaughter, Pamela Tiffin, who is messing around with family pilot Robert Wagner. Wagner in turn is involved with nightclub chanteuse Julie Harris. In his peregrinations toward the dénouement Newman meets an actress who has seen better days, Shelley Winters, and her husband, Robert Webber.

Webber runs a smuggling ring, whose owner is Strother Martin, a religious nut. Harper gets into a variety of dangerous setups, gets beaten up, etc., and the path, to make a long (and often complex and tedious) plot short, leads eventually to family lawyer Graves (Arthur Hill), who had killed the millionaire out of hatred for him and love for Tiffin. He and Newman come to a draw, but because they are friends, Hill doesn't kill him. Anyway, killing off the hero (or anti-hero, rather) is rarely done in films of this sort. Bacall, Shelley Winters, and Harris, compelling as a drug-addicted entertainer, carry off the honors here.

MURDER ON THE
ORIENT EXPRESS

PARAMOUNT   1974

CREDITS

Sidney Lumet *(Director)*; John Brabourne and Richard Goodwin *(Producers)*; Paul Dehn *(Screenplay)*; From the Novel by Agatha Christie; Geoffrey Unsworth *(Photographer)*; Richard Rodney Bennett *(Music)*; Tony Walton *(Production Design and Costumes)*; Jack Stephens *(Art Director)*. Panavision and Technicolor.

CAST

Albert Finney *(Inspector Hercule Poirot)*; Sean Connery *(Col. Arbuthnot)*; John Gielgud *(Beddoes)*; Ingrid Bergman *(Greta Ohlsson)*; Lauren Bacall *(Mrs. Hubbard)*; Richard Widmark *(Ratchett)*; Wendy Hiller *(Princess Dragomiroff)*; Vanessa Redgrave *(Mary Debenham)*; Michael York *(Count Andrenyi)*; Jacqueline Bisset *(Countess Andrenyi)*; Anthony Perkins *(Hector McQueen)*; Martin Balsam *(Bianchi)*; Jean-Pierre Cassel *(Pierre Michel)*; George Coulouris *(Dr. Constantine)*; Rachel Roberts *(Hildegarde Schmidt)*; Colin Blakely *(Hardman)*; Denis Quilley *(Foscarelli)*.

Opened at the Coronet Theatre, New York, November 24, 1974. Running time, 127 minutes.

Bacall has written of *Murder on the Orient Express:* "Along came Sidney Lumet with an offer for [the film] with a blinding cast of star actors. So one English year was to stretch into two. With that film experience came not only new friendships but the happiest work experience I'd had in my movie life since the beginning."

Bacall is a capricious American, here with Wendy Hiller, **Rachel Roberts**, Sean Connery, Anthony Perkins and Martin Balsam.

Holding the sinister knife.

Bacall is questioned about a knife—a possible murder weapon.

There was considerable admiration for Bacall's work in this fascinating Paul Dehn screenplay based on the novel by the Grand Lady of Mystery Thrillers, Agatha Christie. Respect for Bacall's contribution was all the greater considering the cast she was up against, including Ingrid Bergman, who won a Best Supporting Actress Oscar for *her* work in it, John Gielgud, Wendy Hiller, Richard Widmark, Anthony Perkins, Sean Connery, Vanessa Redgrave, and with that excellent actor Albert Finney losing his identity completely in that of the legendary detective, Hercule Poirot.

Bacall's was the character of a famous American actress travelling incognito under her married name, Mrs. Hubbard. She is vulgar, garrulous, expensively dressed, vital enough but afflicted with a "Betty Brillo"-type personality. Her role was best defined by the British critic Benny Green, who wrote of it in *Punch:* "Mrs. Hubbard is a rich American, and the living proof of Oscar Wilde's theory that America went from barbarism to decadence without the intervening stage of civilization."

While there will be many to disagree with Green's (and Wilde's) analysis of the American character, reminding the British that they have had their own flourishing periods of both barbarism and decadence, there is no denying the negative force of Bacall's portrait here. She seems to have given much thought to the role and just how it was to be gotten across, and her dress, manners, expressions, gestures, and stances illuminate her character vividly and expertly.

Once, when congratulated by a journalist on her standout performance here, she generously commented, "The thanks belong in part to my acting associates on the picture. Now I ask you, how could anyone not want to give of his-her best when put up against some of the finest talents of this century?"

Listening tensely with the others.

Certainly *Murder on the Orient Express* was a stylish, handsome, beautifully mounted production, with screenwriter Dehn capturing every value Christie had inserted into the original, and Sidney Lumet in top form guiding, as he did, such a variegated collection of talents. Geoffrey Unsworth caught the 1934 Orient Express ambience extremely well, and Tony Walton, who did the costumes and production design, imparted to each performer a unique representation of an individual persona. Praise also is due art director Jack Stephens, and this was one case in which the elaborately-placed-and-focussed Technicolor and Panavision effects enhanced a period piece rather than detracted from it.

The plot, intricate and with a delightful surprise dénouement, is Agatha Christie at her most inventive and clever. On the Orient Express circa 1934 are a varied assortment of characters travelling from Istanbul to Calais. They include Richard Widmark, a wealthy American with underworld connections; his grovelling secretary, Anthony Perkins; Sean Connery, a retired army officer, and his fiancée, Vanessa Redgrave; Michael York, a young aristocrat madly possessive of his young wife, Jacqueline Bisset; a Swedish missionary, Ingrid Bergman, who has an unbalanced religiosity; Miss Bacall, whose character has already been delineated; and detective Poirot, who has won fame in his native France and elsewhere for his deductive skills, applied with eminent success to solving a variety of tricky cases.

Widmark is murdered after being drugged; he is stabbed twelve times in the chest. Poirot, given Widmark's unsavory past as an underworld associate, theorizes that he was the victim of a Mafia murder, but gradually comes to suspect that the passenger roster contains the murderer. After intensive questioning, he learns that each of the twelve had been involved, one way or another, with the family of a child whom Widmark, in his unsavory criminal past, had kidnapped and murdered.

In the startling conclusion, Finney comes to realize that Widmark had been stabbed by each passenger in turn, after being drugged by his valet, John Gielgud, in a ritual revenge murder for the original crime. But railroad official Martin Balsam persuades the detective to report to authorities that it was a Mafia crime, in order to save the railroad's and the famous passengers' good name.

OE - 2123

Poirot zeroes in on Perkins while the others watch: Jean-Pierre Cassel, Vanessa Redgrave, Connery, Ingrid Bergman, George Coulouris, Rachel Roberts, Wendy Hiller, Denis Quilley, Michael York, Jacqueline Bisset, Bacall and Martin Balsam.

THE SHOOTIST

PARAMOUNT-DINO DE LAURENTIS   1976

CREDITS

Don Siegel *(Director)*; M.J. Frankovich and William Self *(Producers)*; Miles Hood, Glendon Swarthout, Scott Hale *(Screenplay)*; Based on the novel by Glendon Swarthout; Bruce Surtees *(Photographer)*; Elmer Bernstein *(Music)*; Robert Boyle *(Production Designer)*; Dino De Laurentiis *(Production Company)*; Douglas Stewart *(Editor)*; Technicolor.

CAST

John Wayne *(John Bernard Books)*; Lauren Bacall *(Bond Rogers)*; Ron Howard *(Gillom Rogers)*; James Stewart *(Dr. Hostetler)*; Richard Boone *(Mike Sweeney)*; Hugh O'Brian *(Pulford)*; Bill McKinney *(Cobb)*; Harry Morgan *(Marshal Thibido)*; John Carradine *(Beckum)*; Richard Lenz *(Sam Dobkins)*; Sheree North *(Serepta)*; Scatman Crothers *(Moses)*; Gregg Palmer *(Burly Man)*; Kathleen O'Malley *(Schoolteacher)*.

Opened at the Astor Plaza Theatre, New York, August 11, 1976. Running time, 100 minutes.

Bacall was reunited with John Wayne for what turned out to be his final picture, *The Shootist* (1976). It was shot from January to March of that year, with location filming in Carson City, Nevada. Wayne plays an aging gunfighter who in the year 1901—already in the wrong century—comes to a Nevada town to die. Cancer is eating away at him, and a doctor (James Stewart in a cameo role) advises him to die a suicide with dignity rather than endure the terminal pain.

She is touching as a landlady with a human side.

Bacall's initial coldness becomes warmth.

179

Her concern for the old gunman grows.

Wayne elects to die with dignity all right—in a terminal gunfight in a bar with enemies facing him. He outshoots them all but dies at the hands of the bartender. The bartender is promptly dispatched in his turn by Wayne's young admirer, Ron Howard—who then throws away the gun as if to indicate that he will never fire another one. The ideals that Wayne represent—if they can be termed ideals—thus fail to survive him.

The action takes place during the week that followed the death of Queen Victoria, as if to indicate that 1901 was indeed the Year of Anachronisms Who Lived Too Long—both in London and in the Old West.

Bacall plays a landlady who rents a room to Wayne. At first she is coldly hostile, repelled by his murderous reputation and fearful that he will set a pernicious example to her impressionable son, Howard. But gradually she warms to him, recognizing as she does, the lonely valor of his preparation for The End. And when he sets out on his Last Journey to the bar where he will meet his Fate, the audience has the partial gratification—call it catharsis, then—of knowing that he carries Bacall's affection and concern—however belated—with him.

This Wayne valedictory is particularly poignant because he made it during respites from bouts with the cancer that dogged his own last years, and eventually killed him three years later. Wayne had plans to make other films in the 1976-79 period, but could not muster the ultimate physical strength and purpose required. *The Shootist* is a fitting farewell to the screen for Wayne, with its touching implication that the Great Macho Conservative of films—*and* America—had also outlived the great fame on screen, complete with 1969 Oscar for *True Grit,* that had been his for so long. "True Grit" certainly describes Wayne's characterization in this film, as in the final years of the private man.

Ron Howard is touching as the youngster who admires Wayne, and takes revenge on his murderer, but who signifies, in throwing away his gun, his own refusal to carry on an older tradition.

Bacall was 51 when she did this film, her first in two years, and in her severe neck-high 1901 dresses and upswept hairdo she cannot be said to represent the flamboyant Bacall of legend. Her manner is severe and dourly authoritative, but her character softens, at first subtly but then more poignantly and perceptibly, as she comes to realize that her dying but still feisty boarder has more than one dimension to him, and contains within himself all the complex facets of a human personality, good and bad. And Bacall limns tellingly her eventual realization of the man's essential courage in the face of the Last Enemy any human being comes to know.

It must have been a poignant experience for Bacall, the making of a film in which her eminent co-star was himself in the midst of a cancer siege—the same disease that had killed her first husband, Bogart, nineteen years before. And it saddened her mightily to note Wayne's deterioration, at age 69, from the vigorous 48-year-old she had acted with twenty-one years before in *Blood Alley.*

But in this more mature, graver, sadder final period, with both stars no longer young, it is interesting to note that the mutual star-chemistry is still intact, though pictorially altered. Wayne had just completed a picture with Katharine Hepburn (*Rooster Cogburn)* and *their* chemistry had *also* proved compelling.

A bevy of fine supporting actors help sustain the ambience of this poignant Western swan-song for Wayne, among them Richard Boone, Hugh O'Brian, Harry Morgan, and Scatman Crothers. Don Siegel, the director, managed to turn in a good picture despite his frequent clashes with Wayne, who by then was old and ill and couldn't tolerate direction,

Bacall is concerned that son Ron Howard will take the gunman as a role-model.

and who insisted on changes that irritated Siegel.

This is hardly a co-starring spot for Bacall; her role could be defined more as a strong supporting one. *The Shootist* will always be viewed primarily as John Wayne's farewell to the screen, but Bacall makes a creditable contribution nonetheless.

Howard Kissel wrote of her in *Women's Wear Daily:* "Lauren Bacall is strong as the wise landlady." In *The New York Times,* Frank Rich said she was "miscast as a pious schoolmarm type…doesn't fit into Wayne's universe," while Kathleen Carroll in the New York *Daily News* opined: "[She] gives a performance of surprising complexity."

THE FAN

PARAMOUNT   1981

CREDITS

Edward Bianchi *(Director)*; Kevin McCormack *(Executive Producer)*; Priscilla Chapman and John Hartwell *(Screenplay)*; Based on the novel by Bob Randall; Dick Bush *(Photographer)*; Color by Technicolor; Pino Donaggio *(Music)*; Alan Heim *(Editor)*.

CAST

Lauren Bacall *(Sally Ross)*; James Garner *(Jake Berman)*; Maureen Stapleton *(Belle Goldman)*; Michael Biehn *(Douglas Breen)*; Hector Elizondo *(Ralph Andrews)*; Anna Maria Hosford *(Emily)*; Kurt Johnson *(David)*; Feiga Martinez *(Elsa)*; Reed Jones *(Choreographer)*.

Opened at Loew's State, Loew's New York Twin, 34th Street Showplace and other theatres, May 21, 1981. Running time, 95 minutes.

Signing autographs for admirers.

After a five-year absence from the screen, Bacall returned in a role that was a highly flamboyant contrast to her prim, starchy, reserved landlady of 1901 vintage in *The Shootist.* In *The Fan,* based on the lurid shocker by Bob Randall which did well on the bookstalls, Bacall is very much a 1981 lady, here on display as a stage star very like her true stage self. She finds herself stalked by a handsome but quite deranged young man, Michael Biehn, who is a living illustration of all that public personalities dread about the worst, most sinister aspects of star adoration and obsessiveness.

Most of the 1981 reviewers did not quite know what to make of the film, with some of them waxing good-natured and calling it good campy fun and

Bacall is repelled by the letters.

others labeling it a cheap and vulgar exploitation film disguised by Bacall's star charisma and some fancy production values.

James Garner is on hand as Bacall's ex-hubby who proves himself a pillar of strength, courtesy of the ever-more-loony Biehn, and Maureen Stapleton is Bacall's secretary, who writes curt impersonal rejoinders to Biehn's adoring missives—and gets a thorough knifing in the subway for her pains. Ditto (though not in the subway but in the YMCA pool) a handsome young associate of Bacall's who incurs homicidal Biehn's unreasoning jealousy when he is seen by him with the star.

Things get thicker and thicker and ever more turgid and turbulent as Biehn grows more threatening, and since Stapleton has not kept the addresses on his letters, he continues to be unknown, unlocated, and unidentified. But soon detective Hector Elizondo is hot on the case, making already-jittery star Bacall more and more nervous by indicating that she may be next on the knifing list. The letters grow increasingly manic and sinisterly threatening, and shortly Biehn is invading her apartment and slashing her posters and other belongings.

All ends in a gotterdammerung at the theatre, where musical comedy star Bacall has opened in her new offering, and there is Biehn, done up in black tie, sitting right in the audience. Later, in a darkened theatre, comes the final confrontation, with *Bacall* wielding a knife for a change, and plunking her tormentor, stone-dead, into an orchestra seat where he stares sightlessly at the stage while Bacall rushes for the exit—liberated at long last.

Edward Bianchi directed these melodramatic, screamy doings in a melodramatic, screamy style. Fine actress Maureen Stapleton tries to inject some pungency and humor into the proceedings, as

The star relaxes at a party.

A moment of high tension.

Garner tenders a needed boost.

Detective Elizondo discusses letters with Bacall and Garner.

Bacall's secretary-pal, but only partially succeeds in overcoming the cheapie techniques running rampant. But the scene where the crazed fan stalks her in the subway has its share of suspense and terror—looking better than it actually is, being surrounded by so much shabbiness in situations and characterizations.

James Garner is just along for the ride in a basically supporting role as the concerned, standby ex-husband. As for Michael Biehn, he is handsome in a menacing way, callowly nauseating in his unreserved admiration of his idol, and sneaky and sinister as all get out when he goes on his terminal (for him) super-rampage. His character waxes inventive in a crazy way, as he murders and then burns a gay guy he has picked up, and passes the unrecognizable body off as his own, thus leading Bacall and Garner to imagine that the danger is over.

The picture should have catapulted the intense and not ungifted Biehn into a respectable career of screen leads, but he has been little heard from since (last time I saw him, he was a particularly nasty cadet in *Lords of Discipline*). Possibly the unwholesome sick-sick quality inherent in the role typed him in current producers' minds as a poor man's Peter Lorre of the 1980s; hopefully he can survive such stereotyping.

As for Bacall, she profits from her association with such hit musicals on Broadway as *Applause* (1970) and *Woman of the Year* (1981), so her appearance here as a top Broadway musical star has real-life authenticity. Oddly, as photographed by Dick Bush and directed by Bianchi, her actual musical appearances are perfunctory and undistinguished—possibly because their presentational techniques belong more to stage than screen. Bush has presented and lighted her attractively, considering that she was 56 when she made the film; luckily for Bacall, even her lines and bulges fit the current public conception of her. But the picture was garish and cheap, for all the production efforts expended, and all in all, was an unworthy vehicle for the 1981 Bacall.

Going over matters with secretary, Stapleton.

F-66-3

Michael Biehn plots fresh mischief.

Biehn gets nasty with his idol's portrait.

William Schoell in *Quirk's Reviews* wrote of *The Fan:* "Closeups of razors cutting into Maureen Stapleton's cheeks, a pool filling up with diluted red blood, are gory and sensationalistic images, but they aren't enough to give the picture the class or energy that it desperately needs. Furthermore, the choppy continuity is only made more apparent [instead of being disguised] by the blackouts that fill the screen and stop the action dead between each scene.... Bacall is an engaging personality, the production values are reasonably good, and Bacall croaks out a nice number before the film's climax."

Variety said: "Lauren Bacall makes the film work with a solid performance. To be sure, the part doesn't test the broadest range of [her] abilities, but she [and the director] achieve the essential element: they make the audience care what happens to her." And from Ernest Leogrande in The New York *Daily News:* "The direction, camera work and use of locales capture the Manhattan settings and show business milieu with admirable accuracy... suspenseful and intelligent as the approach is, though, the movie comes across primarily as Grand Guignol, a documentation of ugly occurrences in which madness is simply presented, not psychologically explored."

The star defies her deranged tormentor.

HEALTH

20TH CENTURY-FOX   1982

Garner tries to resuscitate "suspended" Bacall while a
hapless young woman watches.

CREDITS

Robert Altman *(Producer-Director)*; Robert Altman, Frank Barhydt, and Paul Dooley *(Screenplay)*; Edmond Koons *(Photographer)*; Dennis M. Hill *(Film Editor)*; Bob Gravnor *(Sound)*; A 20th Century-Fox release.

CAST

Lauren Bacall *(Esther Brill)*; Carol Burnett *(Gloria Burbank)*; Glenda Jackson *(Isabella Garnell)*; James Garner *(Harry Wolff)*; Dick Cavett *(Himself)*; Paul Dooley *(Harold Gainey)*; Donald Moffat *(Colonel Cody)*; Henry Gibson *(Bobby Hammer)*; Diane Stilwell *(Willow Wertz)*; MacIntyre Dixon *(Fred Munson)*; Alfre Woodard *(Sally Benbow)*; Ann Ryerson *(Dr. Ruth Ann Jackie)*; Allan Nicholls *(Jake Jacobs)*; Margery Bond *(Daisy Bell)*; Georgann Johnson *(Lily Bell)*; Mina Kolb *(Iris Bell)*; Bob Fortier *(Henderson)*; Nancy Foster *(Gilda)*; and the Steinettes *(Julie Janney, Diane Shaffer, Nathalie Blossom, Patty Katz)*.

Opened at the Film Forum Theatre, New York, April 7, 1982. Running time, 96 minutes.

The self-indulgent Robert Altman had himself a sleazily disorganized field day with *Health*, which he directed *and* produced for 20th Century-Fox in 1979. A satire on the American craze for physical fitness, set at a health-food convention (of sorts) in one of those 1920s Spanish-style Florida hotels that in latter years have survived via taking business of this kind, *Health* is a mess from start to finish, and unintelligible and pointless to boot. It has Bacall on hand playing—are you ready?—a virgin of 83 who claims she has stayed fit for eight decades by

Bacall (when not in suspended animation) says "Hi" to Carol Burnett, while Dick Cavett concentrates on playing Himself—who else?

foregoing even one orgasm. She is running for president of *Health,* a national group with political clout, and her campaign manager, Jim Garner, has, among his other redoubtable tasks, the major assignment of shielding from her "public" the fact that she falls prey to suspended animation when tired or indisposed.

Now there were comic possibilities in this situation, but Altman does not explore them. He merely repeats Bacall's arm-stiffly-raised, expression-endlessly-held bouts until they grow tedious. Nor does he make the most of the talented Carol Burnett's graceless but potentially larkish role as the President's representative, who keeps declaring that the All-Highest in the White House is definitely for Health—and who also happens to be Garner's ex-wife. Then there's Glenda Jackson, the best actress in the lot (when the right director [not Altman] permits her to be). Here she's Bacall's fanatically humorless rival—a health nut of the worst kind.

Dick Cavett is on hand as himself—watching the Johnny Carson show during hours off. People go around disguised as various forms of vegetable—carrot, tomato, you-name-it. Nothing much happens as all get to do their "star-turn." The minimal plot turns—actually only hooks for sight gags and subliminal stuff that doesn't make points clearly—have to do with who gets elected, and we are treated to a variety of weirdos, health freaks, and commercial-minded types in boyishly mischievous pursuit of the American Dream—in this case the "Health"-racket. Garner's feeble efforts to win back Burnett are thrown in almost as an afterthought, for a romantic fillip (a weak-tea one.)

For many years now, Altman has been getting away with murder in pictures like this. His very own specialty seems to be the disguising of his chronic inability to tell a story clearly. He usually throws in a lot of "free-flowing," "free-association" damned-foolishness that some critics mistake for highly individual "art." What is sad about *Health* is that all the potentially funny situations are distinctly un-

funny from start to finish.

Health has had a strange history. It was made for 20th Century-Fox release in 1979. Then came one of those ever-recurring changes of studio management. *Pro-Health*ers claim that the new bosses had declared the film unreleasable trash in order to make their predecessors look bad. The Anti-*Health*ers insisted that the new boys in power were damned right in burying it. In any event, the picture was not seen by beast nor man until 1980, did not get a New York release until 1982, and has played to puzzled TV audiences who for the most part can make neither head nor tail of it.

The movie picked up a certain cult among those film critics who adore obscurantist nonsense that plays jokes on the public by pretending to sly profundities and satirical pointedness that is not evident in the product to either fool, or wise man. No-nonsense reviewers like the New York *Daily News's* Ernest Leogrande, however, "told it like it was," with Leogrande observing: "What Altman and his two co-writers have achieved suggests an extended skit in a college fraternity show."

Bacall does what she can with the role of the octogenarian given to suspended animation at awkward times, but neither Altman's direction nor the script help her to get across any true or sharp comic effects. This is a shame, because Bacall's potential for wry and witty commentary is always evident, and the fact that her colleagues have not provided her with opportunities to exploit it is regrettable in the extreme. If the film had been up to the standard of her always-evident possibilities, *Health,* made two years before but released one year after her starring vehicle *The Fan,* might have opened the way for a major Bacall Film Renaissance. But it was not to be.

Aside from the observations of prominent film critics who should know better but who insist on declaring their adoration of such nonsense, *other* observations from *honest* reviewers ranged from "uneven" to "incomprehensible" to "thoroughly unfunny."